An insider's guide to
Skopelos

by
Maria Broadley

Published by Travelleur Publishing
Denby Dale

First published in 2010 by
Travelleur
96 Thorpes Avenue
Denby Dale
Huddersfield HD8 8TB
UK

ISBN 978-0-9556288-5-6

Printed and bound in Greece by
Printing Company, Georgiadis S.A.

The author has carefully researched all the information for this guide, but no responsibility can be accepted for any unforeseen circumstances encountered whilst following it. However, should you have any problems or find material changes to the information contained in this guide the publisher would be grateful for this information.

Front cover picture: Aghios Ioannis to Kastri (Mamma Mia! Church)

Acknowledgements

My thanks are due to all the clients of Sunvil and GIC, without whom the need for this book would have gone unrecognised; Machi, who has checked telephone numbers and factual information; Sean and Helen Greenhalgh, who have turned hand drawn sketches into real maps; Peter, who has taken the photographs; and to our friends and neighbours on Skopelos, especially Peggy and Lefteris and their family, who have instilled in me a commitment to raising awareness of the traditions, culture and environment of their lovely island home.

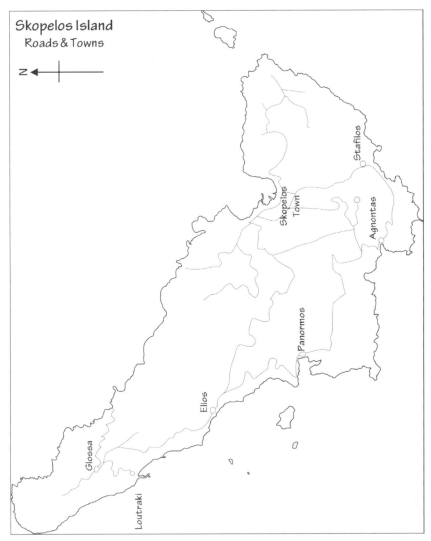

Skopelos Island
Roads & Towns

N

Stafilos
Skopelos Town
Agnontas
Panormos
Elios
Glossa
Loutraki

LIST OF MAPS

Contents

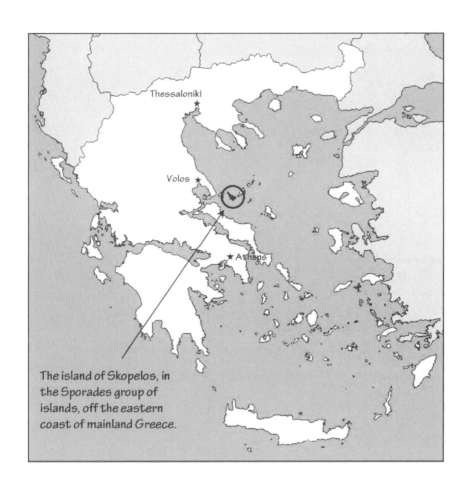

The island of Skopelos, in
the Sporades group of
islands, off the eastern
coast of mainland Greece.

MAP OF GREECE SHOWING
SKOPELOS

Getting to Skopelos

If the visitor who is tired of urban life wants rest and relaxation on the beautiful beaches of Skopelos, he will certainly have a good time, but such a visitor will not get to know the island or understand much of the life of its people. He will be left with an impression of a pine-clad island with beautiful scenery - but anyone who has seen 'Mamma Mia!' will have that.

So why come to Skopelos, an island without an airport, in a cul de sac that can only be approached by sea, (and therefore not on frequent travel routes) with all the inconvenience that being at the mercies of the weather and the vagaries of the ferry companies bring?

There are two reasons already! Getting here is an adventure in itself; one well rewarded by your first glimpse of the town from the open sea, with its striking Byzantine churches crowning the sheer cliffs as you round the headland.

More popular islands take charter planes and many beaches are busy. Ferries get you off the main tourist trail and to the more peaceful and sleepy Greek island holiday.

Skopelos actually has something for almost everyone. It will especially appeal to anyone who loves any of the following: Unspoilt nature; eclectic choice of bars and cafes; crystal clear seas; seaside tavernas; clean air scented with pines; scenic hillside hamlets; shops selling handmade ceramics and jewellery; tiny churches and mountain monasteries; walking trails; pristine isolated coves; family beaches with traditional tavernas... in short it is an island which almost all fall in love with, and which many return to again and again.

So, the real answer is simple. Come to Skopelos and find something that is fast disappearing elsewhere in Greece - the true experience of Hellas.

Skopelos is the capital of the group of islands in the North Eastern archipelago known collectively as the Sporades - that is Skiathos, Alonissos, Skopelos and Skyros - which lie to the east of Volos in the North Aegean Sea, belonging to the province of Magnesia.

Approximately 35 kilometres in length, and covering 96 square Kms, Skopelos lies on the same latitude as Paxos, Majorca, Ibiza and the Azores. A beautiful verdant island, it is very mountainous, the tallest peak being Mount

Delfi at a height of 680 metres. The coastline is varied, with many inlets, and it totals over 60 kilometres.

The climate of Skopelos is Mediterranean, with a wet winter and dry summer. The average annual temperature is 17°C and the average rainfall is about 515mm. As can be seen, Skopelos enjoys a fair amount of rain over the year, which helps to maintain its extensive forests. The winter months of December, January and February are when most of this rainfall comes, and some years there is even snow. Amongst the damp, cold days, there are some warmer periods: in January, there is usually a two week period of pleasant sunny days known as 'Alkyonides' (See the section on myths and legends).

The temperatures of the coldest months from November to March range between 8 to 11°C. The climate is rainy from November to February, March is unpredictable and April can be both rainy and sunny.

March in Skopelos 'comes in like a lion and goes out like a lamb'. Winds mean power fluctuations and sometimes power cuts! A south wind is warm, but brings dust from the Sahara, so windows are never clean.

If the wind is from the North East, then the sea in the main harbour at Skopelos Town is choppy and difficult for boats to access; but the island of Alonnisos protects the south of the island, so the harbour of Agnontas, which is on the lee side, is calm and the journey to Skiathos is positively placid. However, the population and their visitors have the inconvenience of having to cross the island to meet the boats, before returning to town by road. The harbour at Agnontas is extremely small, so if it has to handle more than one boat at a time, the situation can appear chaotic and some delay is to be expected. People here realise that the priorities are boat schedules and island supplies, with passengers down the list, so please be patient! Even so, it is extremely rare to have to wait longer than half an hour.

If the wind is from the North West, then not only is it cold, but waves blown from that direction meet at the bottlenecks of the straits between the Sporades islands, creating huge waves on occasion as the water squeezes between the gaps and making travel into port extremely difficult.

We are an island people and pride ourselves on our resilience. And true travellers will also understand and accept the vagaries of the weather - after all, it is part of what makes Skopelos unique as a tourist destination!

March is also the time to protect oneself from the vagaries of fate. You will often see children, pregnant women and devout young people wearing thin red and gold cords around their left wrists during this month. At Easter weekend, these are taken off and burned with ceremony in the church.

April has the advantage of being a lot warmer, perhaps not for swimming, but at least for sun bathing on the beaches. During the winter and spring months, the south and west beaches are known for having temperatures that are above the ones of the town. From March onwards, the days start to become milder, and wildflowers bloom in abundance.

Summer is usually defined as May through to October. In general, Skopelos' climate is hot in summer, though due to the island's forests the heat is always bearable. Summer weather starts in May or June, with hot sunny days, warm seas, and pleasant evenings. The hottest month of the year is usually July.

August enjoys frequent cooling 'Meltemia'- Northerly winds which start to blow in the evenings, and calm down after lunchtime the following day. The cool and soothing breezes accompany the rising heat. When these welcome summer winds blow, a light sweater is often advisable in the evening.

Skopelos is a mountainous island and you will always find plenty of sheltered beaches, no matter from which direction the wind blows. For example you may try southern beaches when there is a north wind, or vice versa. Those who enjoy 'big ocean' and surf type waves, should try the northern beaches on a northerly-wind day.

Even in summer two or three showers will cool the land and wash the pine forests that stretch down to the blue green coastline on the west and south side of the island.

In September, and October, the evenings start to cool down, and there might be a few showers or cloudy days. November can be varied, with a mix of autumnal/wintry weather. This is the olive picking season, followed by oranges, lemons and walnuts. The islanders work frenziedly to harvest their crops through the winter.

Travelling to Skopelos can be done by various methods:

By Boat

Flying Dolphin/Flying Cat - Hellenic Seaways (hydrofoils and catamarans)

These depart all year round from the mainland ports of **Aghios Constantinos** which lies approximately 260Kms north of Athens, and from the more northern city of **Volos**. Hydrofoils run twice daily (once on Sunday) from Volos to Skiathos, Skopelos, Alonissos and back). It takes approximately 145mins to Skopelos.

There are also inter-island connections between **Alonnisos** and **Skiathos**, although these are not as frequent as they used to be.

Flying Dolphins are for foot passengers only, and are a fast way to travel to and from Skopelos - journey time (2 hours) is usually half that of the ferry boats.

All the Flying Dolphins and catamarans are non-smoking throughout and there are WC facilities on board.

Children aged 5-10 years inclusive travel at approximately half price, whilst children up to age 5 years travel free of charge.

Skopelos ferry boat - Hellenic Seaways

The Express Skiathos services the **Volos** route throughout the season. Journey time is 4 hours.

It can take both cars and foot passengers. There is a cafe-bar on board serving drinks and snacks, WC facilities and plenty of open deck space. This is the way to travel if you have the time! You may be lucky and see dolphins following the ferry and playing in the wake of the boat – marvellous!

Speed Cat 1 - Hellas Speed Cat (High Speed Catamaran ferry)

Speed Cat operates the high speed catamaran **Speed Cat 1** in the summer and offers a daily high speed ferry service from the port of Volos to the islands of Skiathos, Skopelos, Alonnisos and to Aghios Kostantinos on the mainland. Speed Cats are for foot passengers only and are much bigger than the Dolphins. You cannot travel outside the cabins.

NEL line ferry - ANEK LINES

NEL Lines is currently the leading Greek car passenger ferry for all destinations in the North-eastern Aegean. The ship Panagia Thalassini sails from Limnos, Alonissos, Skopelos, Skiathos and Volos; Volos, Skiathos, Skopelos, Skiathos, Volos; and Lavrio, Mesta, Psara, Ag. Eustratios, Limnos, in the summer only.* Restaurants and bars, retail shops and internet access corners are available on board.

Because of the Greek financial difficulties, we still do not have confirmation that this will run regularly at the moment.

By Road and Sea

Athens-Aghios Constantinos:

A shuttle coach is provided from Athens, which departs from the **Alkyon office,** located at **Kaningos Square/Akadimias Street**, up to the port of **Aghios Constantinos**, where you board the boat to the Sporades.

The coach departs approximately 3.5-4 hours prior to departures of the flying dolphins and ferryboats. Places should be reserved at the same time as making ferry/dolphin ticket reservations. There is usually a comfort stop en route for drinks/snacks. This service operates all year round. Hydrofoils run daily except Fri and Sun.

Skiathos, Skopelos, Alonnisos and back - 90mins

Athens – Volos

KTEL runs 9 buses daily from Athens - Volos from Terminal 260 on Liossion St (0030 24210 317186)

OSE runs 5 Athens-Volos buses daily from Larissa Station (0030 2410 567600)

Trains to Volos leave Athens 7 times daily (0030 24210 24056 Volos or phone 0030 1110 for all train enquiries)

NB As Skopelos town is north facing, the seas can occasionally get rough and boats and ferries will divert to the more sheltered harbour at Agnontas on the opposite side of the island.

By Air

Internal flights from **Athens** to **Skiathos** with Olympic run throughout the year. The flight time is 40 minutes, departing from **Eleftherios Venizelos** airport. Reservations for this service can be made directly over the Internet.

From Thessaloniki:

Plans are projected to have a regular sailing from Thessaloniki to Skopelos during the summer months, but there are no details as yet.

By Private Yacht

Departures for sailing the Sporades are normally from Skiathos or Volos, but can also be from Skopelos or Alonissos, with skipper, within the confined charter period with official departure from Skiathos.

Itineraries: for information about sailing areas, please visit:

www.odysseysailing.gr/islands.html

Yachts: please note the skipper should have a room of his own, so for up to 4 guests a 3 cabin yacht will be comfortable.

By Sailing Flotilla

You have the reassurance of being part of a group of like-minded sailors, but with the support of a Lead Crew. You can be as independent as you like, but your Lead Boat Crew are always nearby in case you need any assistance during your trip. They will also recommend the best anchorages, harbours, restaurants and places to visit. There are several holiday companies that offer sailing holidays based on the Sporades, among them **Sunsail** flotilla holidays.

Skopelos Harbour, showing the Paralea

General Information

Skopelos Town

Located on the north east side of the island, Skopelos Town is the main port and municipal center of the island. It is where the ferries and flying dolphin hydrofoils run daily bringing new visitors, mail and supplies to the island. The town is noted for its world architectural heritage status and a walk through the town along the narrow streets and alley ways leading to the Venetian Kastro quarter is well worth the effort.

Skopelos Town is built encircling the harbour and amphitheatrically up the hillside. Built on steep slopes as it is, the centre of town is largely inaccessible by vehicles, but for those staying in the town a car is not a necessity. Most locals use scooters or mopeds to zip up and down the main streets, but the closer you are to the Kastro area, the more difficult it is to go anywhere except on foot.

Viewed from the harbour, it is easy to see that the town is roughly divided into four parts. The oldest part of town extends from the Kastro to the area around sto Christo, above the town hall. It is a warren of dead ends and blind alleys, with tiny houses and chapels piled seemingly haphazardly together. This area was part of the defences of the Kastro itself (see Kastro).

The next area extends to Giftorema, or Gypsy Brook, the green valley which used to be the place where the itinerant metal workers made the balconies and gates for the town. The houses here are bigger and influenced by the architecture of Thessaly and Macedonia.

The main architectural characteristic is the local-stone built roof, formerly used in most houses. This grey coloured stone is a perfect material for houses so well adapted with the environment of the area. However, it has become prohibitively expensive so many new roofs are now tiled. Balconies are traditionally made of wood and several houses retain the old toilet box situated upstairs outside.

The exterior walls of these houses are up to a metre thick, which keeps the building warm in winter and cool in summer. Many of these houses could be termed mansions and many were built by sea captains in the 18th century.

Next, we come to the u-shaped high street, with some great shops to browse in. More recent buildings intersperse with older houses, much bigger and with an enclosed yard, reflecting the increasing prosperity of the island in the 19th century. There are also occasional large, stone square houses in the

Venetian style to be found, strategically placed and easily fortified should the town be attacked. A fine example of this kind of house is near the church with the clock tower (Fanamerini).

Finally, as we walk down towards the port, we come to the bustling harbourside, almost cosmopolitan with its cafes, bars and tavernas, sheltered by mulberry trees. From here, we see the new tourist buildings extending round the bay.

Skopelos has something for everyone: tranquil small squares with marvellous views, quaint churches in magnificent settings or bustling bars with loud music. Its traditional architecture makes it unique amongst Greek islands: Narrow flower-filled cobbled streets climb the hillside between white washed houses with slate or red-tile roofs and bougainvillea cascading down their walls, creating a lovely picture.

Places to see around Skopelos Town

Mount Delfi

Mount Delfi is the highest point on Skopelos, 680 metres above the sea level. It is worth climbing the steps of the old fire observation tower for the superb view, although the walk to Mount Delfi is fairly arduous.

Palouki and its Monasteries

Mount Palouki is 546 metres high. There are several old monasteries here that are worth visiting. The Monastery of the Annunciation is the one that can be seen from Skopelos Town. It belongs to the Xeropotamos Monastery of Mt. Athos and was restored in 1712. On the opposite side is the Monastery of the Transfiguration of the Lord. It was built in the late 15th century and is surrounded by olive and fruit trees. On the western side there is an old threshing floor. Continuing upwards, there are the Monasteries of Ag. Barbara, built in 1648 and St. John the Baptist, founded in 1612. Today this is occupied by nuns, who produce lovely hand-woven articles. The scenery in this area is particularly beautiful. One may tour the mountain by car, but it is even more enjoyable when explored by foot.

Stafilos

West of Palouki spreads the fertile Stafilos valley, which reaches as far as the northern outskirts of Skopelos Town. It was here that the Greek government offered to build an island airport, as it is the only flat piece of land big enough, only to have the islanders refuse. The airport was then built on Skiathos instead.

Drakondoschisma

At the southern tip of the island is Drakondoschisma (Schism of the Dragon), where legend has it that Ag. Righinos slew the dragon which had been causing terror to the people of the island. The dragon fell to its death in the sea and this caused the cliff to divide. Today you can walk to the cliff edge and look down at the sheer drop to blue waters below. Drakondoschisma can be reached by taking the first dirt track to the left after Stafilos, on the way to Agnontas, about half way between the two places (See Dragon myth).

Agnontas

Agnontas was named after the Peparithan winner of the Olympic Games, Agnon. This athlete, who won a race in the Games of 569BC, landed on this beach on the way home and his compatriots, wishing to honour him, gave the place his name. Today, the lovely bay has a small shingle beach and a deep harbour. It is used as an alternative port when the sea is rough and makes it impossible to disembark at Skopelos Town. It is extremely pretty and an ideal spot to catch the sunset at the small café. There are several tavernas here, which serve excellent seafood.

Panormos

As well as having great beach facilities, Panormos is also built on the ancient city of Panormos (7th/8th century BC). It had a fortified citadel on the hill now known as Palaiokastro, the walls of which have been preserved in very good condition. A path leads from here to the cave of the god Pan. Traces of the ancient city can also be made out along the shore.

The pretty beach-side tavernas at the small port of Agnontas

Glossa

Glossa lies 32 km north west of Skopelos town. It is situated on the north-west side of the island, just above Loutraki harbour with an elevation ranging from 200 to 300m. The village faces Skiathos and the mainland. Built in amphitheatrical style, Glossa and its surrounding villages have nearly as many inhabitants as Skopelos Town but the area is more open and spacious. Glossa is an attractive, peaceful village with traditional houses. There is little in the way of shops or commercialism, but you will find a good taverna, a petrol station and also a bank. Glossa adheres strictly to the hours of siesta, so be prepared to find little open between 2.00pm and 6.00pm.

Loutraki

Loutraki is the port of Glossa, the first stop en route from Skiathos to Skopelos and Alonissos. The village is just 28km from the town of Skopelos and 6km from Glossa. Close to Loutraki are the small islands of 'Strogilo', 'Dasia', 'Paximade' and 'Glaronisi'. These four islands play an important role for Loutraki as they act like a natural barrier, protecting the port from bad weather and storms. A little over 300 metres to the west are the interesting ruins of the ancient city of 'Selinounda', as well as parts of a wall from the castle that was located here in the 4th century.

Loutraki continued to be occupied until Roman times. Roman graves, relief marble inscriptions, coins and pots have been discovered here and remains of an old Roman bath-house can be seen at the far end of the waterfront.

Loutraki is a pleasant harbour with a shady tree-lined waterfront. It has all of the shops that you would require for day-to-day supplies and has several tavernas, particularly on the front overlooking the harbour. There is a much better selection of accommodation in Loutraki, with hotel accommodation, rooms to rent and private villas with pools all being available, than in neighbouring Glossa.

Places to see around Glossa town

Elios

Otherwise known as 'New Klima' and built after the evacuation of residents from the old village of Klima. Old Klima suffered extensive damage during the earthquake of 1965. In response to this, Elios was built with government funding and was constructed urgently. More money is being poured into the area, in order to develop the new marina. The town is becoming more attractive as tavernas, cafes and bars open to cater for new visitors. Situated by the coast on the west side of the island, between Milia beach and Klima village, it is 3 km from Klima village, 6 km from Glossa village and 19 km from Skopelos town. The village had 415 inhabitants in the 2001 census.

Klima

The old village of Klima was abandoned by its original inhabitants after the earthquake and landslide of 1965, which also destroyed the old town of Alonnisos, on the neighbouring island. Many of the old houses have been restored, mostly by foreigners. You can enjoy an interesting stroll along the old stony paths to visit the peaceful village with its citrus and olive trees.

Ag. Ioannis Kastri

The views along the road to Ag. Ioannis are magnificent. The little church is built on a small island, now joined to the mainland, on a sheer rock. It is dedicated to St. John the Baptist. If you wish to visit, there are about 200 steps to the top (See Mamma Mia! Church).

The Lighthouse

This is at the most northerly point of the island – Gourounia - and is quite difficult to get to. To reach the lighthouse, you must take a track northwards from Glossa. The track winds its way through the pine trees to the coast where the track bears left along the northern coast. At the end of the track is the magnificent white-washed lighthouse. Here you can enjoy the serenity and peacefulness of the setting and gaze out over the northern Aegean Sea. The lighthouse was built about 40 years ago, after several maritime accidents. No-one lives there now as it is fully automated.

Useful information

Shops

Normally shops are open from around 8.30-13.30 hrs every day except Sundays; also from 17.30-20.00 hrs on Tuesdays, Thursdays and Fridays. Gift shops and kiosks are open every day, with some staying open in the afternoon too.

Newspapers

International newspapers in Skopelos can be bought in a small shop situated directly opposite the port entrance and then first left – the shop is clearly marked 'International Press'. Most publications from the UK are available running a day behind, with some – the Daily Mail, the Express etc - available on the same day.

Newspapers in Glossa are to be had from the kiosk opposite the Church of Kimissis Theodokou in the square where the taxis wait.

If you are staying in Elios, you must go to Skopelos or Glossa for foreign newspapers.

Banks

There are 4 banks in Skopelos town:

- the Commercial, (Emporiki) open only on Thursdays
- the Alpha Bank
- the Agricultural (Agrotiki)
- the National bank (Ethniki)

They are all situated along the main waterfront and are open Monday – Friday 08.00-13.30 hrs. All banks have a cash point machine taking all major credit cards. Other cash point machines are available around town, for example at the bakery directly opposite the port.

For the exchange of travellers' cheques, you will need to show your passport.

'Madro Travel' on the Old Port, Paralea, also change cash and travellers' cheques at the daily bank rate, and are open from 09.00 until approximately 21.30.

The bank in Glossa is situated on the main street on the right hand side as you walk into the centre. There is an ATM machine outside. There is no bank in Elios.

Post Office

The Post office in Skopelos is situated on the right of the street leading from the left of Platanos Square (see Skopelos town map). It is open Monday – Friday 08.00-14.00 hrs. Post boxes are yellow and situated on the waterfront, outside the 'International Press' shop and at the Post office. The cost of a regular weighted letter or post card to the UK is around €1.75. Kiosks and tourist shops often sell stamps with post cards, but will charge a commission.

Telephones

There are public phones all around Skopelos town, especially around the waterfront area. They take phone cards which can be bought from the local kiosk. The price of a telephone card starts at €4. All these telephones are direct dial, so to call the UK just dial **0044** followed by the area code (without the first 0) and finally the telephone number.

Mobile reception can be poor, with dead spots especially at Elios and on the beaches. There are several mobile phone networks operating here; the best reception currently is that afforded by Cosmote. If you dial a local number from your mobile you will probably have to use the international code for Greece, which is 0030.

Although the instructions for the telephones appear in Greek, by pressing the button marked (*i*) you can change the language to English.

E-Mail/Fax

There is an internet cafe in Skopelos Town, at the end of the Paralea at the Old Harbour: The Blue Sea Cafe bar and internet cafe Tel: 0030 24240 23010. There is also Wi-Fi access at cafes in Skopelos Town, Panormos and Glossa - just ask! If you need to send a fax, tourist agencies will probably be able to help you.

Police

The police station on Skopelos is above the National Bank on the Paralea. Let us hope that you never need to visit this establishment! However, should you lose something, you will need to report it to the police if you wish to make an insurance claim. Losses should be reported within 24 hours. You should give the police a description of the lost item. They will then prepare a report and attach the relevant stamps (cost usually less than a euro) ready for you to collect the completed form the next day.

Port Police

In Skopelos Town, the general office is situated at the port itself, and the headquarters is on the road to the T junction, opposite the car hire places. There is an office at Elios and at Loutraki, both of them on the port.

Should you arrive by sailing boat, you will need to contact them here to find out where to berth and pay any fees.

You will need a permit from the port police if you wish to fish from a small boat (no permit is required for fishing from the shore).

Parking fines for illegal parking at the port have to be paid at the main office in Skopelos Town. The current cost is 80 euro.

The Port Police have absolute authority over which vessels can leave the ports of Skopelos Town, Agnontas and Loutraki (Glossa). This includes pleasure craft as well as the commercial ferries, the flying catamarans and hydrofoils. If the wind exceeds, or is predicted to exceed Force 5 on the Beaufort Scale, the hydrofoils will be cancelled and taxi/excursion boats will not be able to leave port. A wind speed of Force 8 will result in the cancellation of the Flying Cats and the ferries also.

If a boat cancellation means that you will miss your flight, you must get an official paper from the port police verifying the cancellation. This paper can be given to your insurance company and may allow reimbursement of any additional costs incurred. Please keep all receipts for extra accommodation, meals and transport.

Fire

Should there be a fire at your accommodation, the primary objectives are to **ensure the safety** of yourself and any members of your party and to alert the relevant authorities. The emergency numbers for the fire brigade and police are **100** and **199** respectively.

Keep calm

- If you are able to extinguish the fire yourself, do so only if you are not putting yourself at risk.
- Do not use water to put out electrical or cooking oil fires.
- Try to isolate the fire by closing doors/windows in the room affected.
- Inform any staff on the premises.
- If there is a telephone, call the local fire service. The number is **100**
- Check room doors for heat or smoke.
- Do not open a hot door. Use an alternative escape route
- Close doors behind you as you leave.
- If smoke is heavy, crawl out, staying close to the floor.
- Take short breaths, if possible through a wet cloth, or hold your breath.
- Leave the property as fast as you can.
- Do not stop for packing, or for personal items. Close doors behind you if you are the last one out.
- Stay away from the building until the fire services allow you to re-enter.

Notes:

If you are trapped in a room, it is often the case that if wet towels are placed around the edge of a closed door (especially the bottom), this will increase its effectiveness as a fire and smoke block.

In smoke filled areas keep your head as low as possible; there is likely to be more breathable air closer to the floor.

If possible, assist others to leave the building but do not put yourself at risk.

Under EOT certification, fire extinguishers supplied are powder based, so are suitable for electric fires.

Please help prevent fire:

By not smoking in bed. In rooms where you do smoke, always check under cushions for smouldering cigarettes and ashes.

Avoid deep fat frying (in self catering accommodation).

Driving on Skopelos

Driving on Skopelos is the best way to see the island; however please be aware that signage is poor and many corners are sharp and not marked. 40Km of good tarmac road link Skopelos town with Stafilos, Agnontas, Limonari, Panormos and, finally, Glossa. From Glossa, a road winds down to the port of Loutraki. There is a road from Skopelos Town past the monastery of Ag. Righinos which comes out between Agnontas and Panormos and a road cutting right across the centre of the island from Glossa almost back to Skopelos Town itself.

Secondary roads provide short cuts to various places; they are unsurfaced, but perfectly navigable with an ordinary car if one drives slowly and carefully. There are also many tracks criss-crossing all over the island. A lot are in very poor condition, but navigable with 4 wheel drive.

The use of seatbelts is required by law and is now being strictly enforced.

Drinking and driving is illegal in Greece, despite any local evidence to the contrary! 'Breath-tests' are continually carried out by the local police.

Petrol

There are 6 petrol stations on the island:

Two in Skopelos town – turn right at the T junction for both;

One on the left of the road leading to Stafilos next to the Supermarket Dia (open 24 hours); One for which you take the road turning right at the T junction on to the ring road, then left from the ring road and on towards the 'industrial heartland' of Skopelos, on the right of the road leading to the monastery of Aghios Righinos; one on the left between Elios and Glossa; one in Glossa.

Opening hours vary from 07:00 until 22:00, although these times may change slightly according to the time of year.

All rental cars now take unleaded petrol, ('aymoleevee' or 'prassino' in Greek), and it is becoming expensive.

Parking

The biggest problem to be encountered is that of parking in Skopelos, Glossa and at any popular tourist destination. Car-parks are few and far between and in the high season are totally inadequate for the number of cars. Be prepared to have to park some distance away from where you want to be, especially in town. You may get away with illegal parking on occasion, but if the police ticket you, there is nothing to do but pay the fine!

Excursions

Compared to other islands, Skopelos is not very commercialized - which is why most people come here! Most people find enjoyment in walking, admiring the scenery, absorbing the sunshine and revelling in the colours around them. If you prefer an abundance of laid-on activities, then Skopelos is not for you. The best way to find information on boat excursions is simply to stroll along the Paralea and check out the boards of the boat captains. For true Greekophiles, we recommend a trip to the Marine Park with Captain Pakis (ask at Madro Travel) and we suggest that you do what the locals do - enjoy the weather, the great food, the conversation and the friendship. You will be glad you came!

Passports

Keep your passport in a safe place. If you should lose your passport, please contact the relevant authorities immediately.

For British Nationals, the British Embassy in Athens is the issuing authority for replacement documents:

As a precaution, make a note of your passport details and keep this separately. Or you can e-mail copies of important documents to yourself before you leave, so that you may access them where ever you are.

Safety

Greece is one of the safest countries in Europe with violent crime and thefts being minimal. It is useful to note that nowadays, bargaining is ineffective and sometimes considered distasteful except in certain souvenir or arts and crafts stores. It is also preferable to avoid speaking against any regional or national political party or soccer team as the Greeks may take offence to it. Taking photographs of military establishments and government locations is strictly prohibited.

Apart from that, when travelling to any unfamiliar environment it is important to stay alert to issues of Health and Safety. Although there are no major health hazards in Greece, as with many other famous tourist destinations there are still some aspects that could be considered potentially hazardous!

Although a member of the EU, not all official health and safety guidelines have filtered through to the more remote areas of Greece and her islands. The same safety standards will not apply as with the rest of the European Union (and certainly not the UK). For those who are aware of this and do not expect the same standards, there are no significant risks - the Greeks have survived quite successfully for years and will no doubt continue to do so!

To ensure that you are well prepared for your holiday here are a few points which may help:

Sunshine

It is advisable to prevent your skin from being exposed excessively to the hot Mediterranean sun as this could result in sunburn or long term skin damage. Ultraviolet sun radiation includes UVA and UVB rays which can cause skin damage, damage to the eyes, thermal exhaustion, thermal shock, photosensitivity or photo allergic dermatitis.

How to prevent sun damage:

- Stay out of the sun between 12.00 and 14.00
- Use sunscreen with a high protection factor, wear sunglasses and a hat
- Drink plenty of fluids
- Use special protective care in the case of children

Greece has a team of helicopter ambulances serving its islands in case of emergency. There is a helicopter pad on Skopelos near Skopelos Town.

Swimming

The beaches and crystal clear waters of Skopelos are perfect for swimming and sunbathing and in order to get the most from your holiday by avoiding discomfort and misfortune, take a few easy precautions.

- Be aware of any strong currents if swimming out to sea
- Ask about the safety of the beaches in terms of jellyfish, urchins, sharp rocks etc.
- If swimming in a secluded location, make sure somebody knows where you are going!
- When snorkelling or boating, wear a T shirt as the reflection of sun on water increases burning potential
- Don't swim for a couple of hours after eating or drinking alcohol

Few swimming pools have covers, fencing or life rings. We advise that all those using swimming pools should take extra care and that children should always be supervised.

Walking

Take plenty of water, suntan lotion and a hat. If you have a mobile, take that as well, although you may have to move around to get a decent reception. Torches are useful if you are walking at night.

Are there any dangerous creatures on Skopelos?

The answer to this question is a definite NO! But if the question is whether there are annoying animals/insects causing discomfort, the answer would have to be yes.

Ants

These can be a problem, so try to ensure that no food is left out in your accommodation. Cover it, put it in a cupboard or, if you have one, the fridge.

Mosquitoes

These may be the biggest pest problem you will encounter in Greece, indoors or out, especially after dark.

The most effective way of keeping the mosquitoes away is simply to close all doors and windows. Close the curtains as well and spray them with mosquito spray. Keep a minimum of lights on in the room. This usually does the trick, but the downside is that it will get very hot inside. A compromise is to wait until after dark, then open the windows and shutters, but close the curtains. You have to make a choice whether to open the doors and windows to let in some cooling air, and the mosquitoes, or keep everything closed with the result being a hot sweaty night, but without mosquitoes.

There is a great range of different mosquito deterrents on offer in supermarkets and chemist shops:

- Electrical devices to plug in the socket with a tablet, or a little container filled with fluids, giving out an evaporating gas that will keep the mosquitoes at bay.

- Mosquito repellent creams and sprays. These are effective, but need to be applied liberally and regularly. If you have a mosquito deterrent that you use at home and works well for you, bring it with you to Greece.

- Mosquito coils are useful if you are outside on your balcony or terrace.

Some people have been known to bring their own mosquito nets. Sounds like a bit of hassle, but you will achieve a good result: mosquito free sleeping space.

NB. Do not scratch bites as they will become inflamed and leave bruising or a scar.

Wasps

What are black and yellow and disliked by all? Answer: Wasps.

They can ruin outdoor dining and socialising, they are really annoying and get in your face and, of course, they sting. The best advice is to sit still and wait for them to go away. However, if you've ever been stung, this is much, much, easier said than done even for adults, let alone toddlers and children and cats and dogs. It also doesn't stop them going in your drink or buzzing around your food.

Generally you are unlikely to get a wasp sting until Autumn, unless you accidentally put your hand or foot on one and they are defending themselves, or unless you disturb a wasp's nest. Up until late July and early August they are busy bringing up and feeding larval wasps, chasing insects, and foraging for food and maintenance materials for the nest. After that their job is mainly done and they gorge themselves on the food they collect, especially on ripe and fermenting fruit; they become more and more dependent on sweet foodstuffs like these and will aggressively seek it out.

Additionally it will be getting hot and very crowded in the nest; the internal temperature of the nest is 5-10°C above the outside temperature, so on a good summer day it can reach 25-30°C inside the nest. On top of this the nest's population is at its highest. It is at this time when they are most likely to sting humans, partly due to bad tempers caused by the heat and overcrowding in the nest, and partly in a semi-drunken reaction to being obstructed in their quest for sweet food.

The sting is the cause of our fear of wasps. Unlike a bee sting, the wasp sting has no barbs and can be used many times.

How to avoid being stung:

- Wasps like bright colours and strong scents, and often will drink moisture from wet towels and clothes, so be careful in handling them.
- Don't walk barefoot.
- If you can, keep still; flapping human arms look quite interesting to wasps.

It is best to avoid killing wasps as they emit a pheromone when dying which acts as a signal to other wasps that they are under attack, and so they will come to the wasp you have just killed to see if they can help him.

Pain from a wasp sting is caused by a complex protein injected through the sting as it penetrates the skin. Individuals react differently: some are hardly affected, others experience pain and swelling, while in other cases again, individuals may suffer serious allergic reactions which can even result in death from anaphylactic shock.

Fortunately, there are many proprietary remedies for wasp stings, which are available from chemists and supermarkets.

What you should always do:

- Wash with soap and water
- Apply anti histamine spray or cream, or take anti histamine tablets unless you are allergic to these treatments. Always check with your pharmacist.
- Apply an ice-pack to reduce swelling - always place a tea towel or similar between the ice pack and the skin

- Seek medical attention if you are susceptible to insect bites generally
- Seek medical attention immediately if you suffer vomiting, diarrhoea, hypotension, fever, convulsions, or momentary loss of consciousness
- Seek medical attention immediately if you suffer rashes, itching, nausea, cramps, severe dizziness or headaches, or are allergic to wasp stings

Incidentally, ancient remedies include a plaster made from wild mallow leaves, bay oil, vinegar and salt mixed with honey, and goose dung!

Remember, as annoying as they are, wasps are very beneficial and interesting insects, with a highly developed social structure. Wasps also do a really good job in the garden and orchard - they cross pollinate flowers and kill aphids. Wasps work really hard during their short lives and maybe deserve a break from their status as the creature we most like to eliminate.

Scorpions

In Greece, there is a scorpion to be found called Mesobuthus gibbosus. Its sting is quite painful, but not life threatening. They are terrestrial and nocturnal, so finding one on your bedroom wall would be a very rare occurrence! They are normally found hidden under stones and other places where it is dark. Avoid walking about in bare feet and shake out any shoes or clothing that has been left outside overnight. If you do get stung, seek medical attention at once.

Pine Processionary Caterpillar

This pest is found nearly everywhere in Greece, from sea level to altitudes of 1800 m on Mount Olympus, during Spring. In addition to attacking all pine tree species, the caterpillar has highly irritating hairs, which if touched introduce a toxin causing skin welts and immense local irritation. Antihistamine treatment is required.

Pollen

The Greek pollen season is at its height from April to June. The pollen from pine trees and olive trees is particularly allergenic. If you suffer from hay fever or asthma, please make sure you have anti-allergenic medication and/ or inhalers. If you have questions or anxieties about the efficacy of medicines, the pharmacists will be happy to offer advice.

Snakes

There are several varieties of snakes on Skopelos, but only one is venomous; the viper. If you go walking in the country, through grass or rocky places, carry a stick and make a noise, then any snakes will get out of your way. You see more in early summer than later on. They love basking in sunny places after the winter.

In the highly unlikely event that you are bitten by a snake, it rarely proves to be fatal, just very uncomfortable - symptoms include severe headache and muscle pains. If bitten, keep calm, avoid exertion and seek medical advice immediately. All pharmacies stock antidotes, or you can go to the nearest clinic, medical centre or doctor.

Sandflies

If you decide to sleep on or near a beach, it is sensible to wear insect repellent to protect against sandflies. These may spread a protozoal infection called leishmaniasis, which is difficult to treat.

Sea Urchins

Sea urchins occur frequently in Skopelos, because the coastal areas are rocky - you do not often find them on sandy beaches. When you go swimming in a rocky area, use beach sandals, and watch your steps carefully!

Should you step on one, try to resist the urge to poke, prod or pick at the spines to get them out. By doing this you will cause swelling and perhaps infection. As soon as possible spread cooking oil over the area. After a while, any quills will be easy to remove. Another efficacious solution is to apply toothpaste!

Sea Anemones

Some sea anemones grow on pebbles in seaweed areas on the waterside. They are small - 10 cm only, but they burn like a stinging nettle when in contact with thin skin - not when you step on it. Don't sit in seaweeds on Skopelos. This can be potentially hazardous to smaller children.

Jelly Fish

Jelly fish can occur periodically in the sea, or washed up on the beach. Moon jellyfish are transparent and harmless, but Cassiopaeia jelly fish can sting. They are about 40 cm in diameter and look like a fried egg with tentacles. There is also a very small, transparent jelly fish, 5-8 cm in diameter, and 10-15 cm tall. It stands upright in the sea, and being transparent, is hard to spot, especially while swimming. They are easier to catch sight of while snorkelling, when you can see them just below the surface. Touching the jellyfish feels like a bite or sting. It 'burns' instantly and quite severely, causing a stinging rash. An Aloe Vera cream/gel is handy to cool down and soften the pain. However, this jellyfish is not numerous.

Stingrays and Skates

These can frequent bays with sandy bottoms, where they bury themselves in the sand. They will lash out with their tails if trodden on, so make your presence known in advance by splashing around when entering the water.

Earthquakes

Skopelos is situated in a high frequency earthquake area. Most earthquakes pass unnoticed but, on average, several tremors per year can be felt.

Regulations have made most buildings safe from all but the strongest 'quakes. Try to resist the temptation to rush outside, as most injuries are caused by falling masonry and roof tiles. The safest place is in the corner of a room, or under an interior door lintel.

Most earthquakes on Skopelos cause little or no damage, but give you an experience to share with your friends when you return safely home!

Finally, the good news – Greece is rabies free!

The sheltered winter harbour of Blo (safe harbour) near Panormos

The view towards Alonnisos and the Marine Park from Mount Palouki

Stafilos bay from the headland

Health Services

On Skopelos we have an excellent health centre, two dental practices and two good pharmacies.

The health centre is situated on the perimeter road leading to the old town or Kastro area. Head away from the old and new ports; at the end of the road turn right; follow the road up the hill. The road will bear left and the medical centre is clearly signed and visible from the road on the right.

The Greek word for Doctor is 'Yatros'. The Greek word for hospital is 'Nosokomio'.

Opening hours are from 08.00-14.00 and 18.00-20.00, but there is usually somebody there in case of an emergency and there is always a doctor on call 24 hours a day.

Privacy and patient confidentiality are relatively unknown, so have someone with you who can attempt to 'run interference' for you if you have any problem of a sensitive nature. Irrespective of how many people are waiting, emergencies and children are given priority.

Dental Practices

There are two dental practices in Skopelos Town:

One (Radamantis) is situated above the International Newsagency and is clearly signposted: Ioannis Radamantis 0030 24240 22862.

The other (Tsarpalas) is to the left of the stepped street leading up from the cake shop Ambrosia on the harbour front, beside the church of Aghios Mikhail Sinadhon: Giorgos Tsarpalas 0030 24240 22208 .

There is usually no need to make an appointment if there is an emergency. Surgeries are open from 09.00-13.00 and from 17.00-21.00. The dentists speak English.

Pharmacies

In Skopelos Town there are two. One is directly opposite the Medical Centre: Tsarpalas 0030 24240 24333.

The other is situated just away from the main waterfront; from the old port walk past the bakery on your right. The road will veer up and slightly right into Platanos Square – you will find the pharmacy on the opposite corner on the right: Radamantis 0030 24240 22666/0030 24240 22252.

The Greek word for pharmacy is "Farmakio". Pharmacists are fully trained to treat minor problems such as topical infections, bites, allergies, cuts and grazes. They will also advise you of the appropriate medication and can often prescribe it for you without the need to go to the Medical Centre. Homeopathic and herbal remedies are also widely available.

Opening hours are usually 09.00-14.00 and 17.00-20.00 daily. In May and September the pharmacies may be closed on Sundays.

Whilst in Greece you will be expected to pay all your medical costs locally. Emergency treatment is usually free, but you have to pay for any medication. Always ask for a receipt as costs may be claimed from your medical insurance on your return to the UK.

Be aware that Codeine is classed as a narcotic drug in Greece, so you cannot buy it.

There is a private doctor in Skopelos Town, whose charges should be covered by medical travel insurance in most cases. He speaks excellent English. In case of medical emergency, he can be contacted on:

Dr I Skaventzos   0030 699 99 24 555

Utilities

Water

Approximately 1000 years BC, the people of ancient Greece made holes in the ground lined with clay, in which they conserved the water which fell in abundance during the winter. This water had to last them through the long summer months. Certainly by 400 BC the Greeks had built sophisticated water reservoirs to serve the villages, and even town communities. It was the Venetians in the 16th century who taught them how to bore deep wells and to construct larger and stronger reservoirs; and it was the Peel Government, in Queen Victoria's reign, which dispatched a team of engineers by sailing ship to Paxos to build the fine stone cisterns which are still in use today.

Here on Skopelos, the sources of the municipal water supply are various spring fed tanks located around the island. The three island communities (Skopelos, Elios and Glossa) supply water within a limited but expanding part of their jurisdiction, whilst homes outside the municipal water system use wells or cisterns to collect rain water.

Private water wells supply some agricultural needs and water from these wells can be transported by lorry to outlying areas to refill cisterns or swimming pools. There are plans to construct an artificial lake in the area of Panormos to supply water to farmers and groundwork has begun.

The municipal water is good quality. As with most natural source water in limestone environments, the water has a high calcium content, but it is perfectly safe and indeed healthy, to drink. If however, you are from a soft water area or live in a densely populated area in your home country, you may not like the taste.

Many Greeks drink the local water and buy bottled water, which they use in their appliances, therefore avoiding the calcifying of their kettles, irons etc. It is also handy to have some bottled water around in the case of power cuts, especially if you are dependent on pumped water.

Construction of a 4,836,400 Euro wastewater treatment plant started in March 2007 and is now fully operational. Until now, sewage from the main towns was minimally treated and pumped into the sea. Even in such a short period, the difference the plant has made in the cleanliness of water in the main harbour in Skopelos Town is amazing.

The settlement at Agnontas has its own wastewater treatment facility which has been operating since 2005.

Pipes in Greece are small bore and in cities like Athens, they still link in with ancient systems. Narrower pipes means easier blockage , even with the new mains sewage network. Homes and hotels outside of the sewage grid use cesspool systems (Vothra). Basically, this is a deep hole lined in a lattice pattern with limestone blocks. This allows a natural soak away and biodegradation of organic waste. If too much paper finds its way into the Vothra, then the pores will become clogged and the natural process impeded. For these reasons, plumbing here, as in most of Greece, remains a little unorthodox. As a general rule, please do not put paper or sanitary items into the toilet, but use the bin provided.

Electricity

The Public Power Corporation (DEH) has to bring electricity from the mainland under the sea to Skiathos, then overland via electricity pylons across the island and back under the sea to Skopelos. The cable comes ashore at Loutraki. This complex system means that power cuts are more frequent than perhaps they would be in UK.

If the power is off at 8.00 am the chances are that work is being carried out by the state electricity company.

If the power should go off at any other time, the first step is to check the fuse box. Turn off all appliances, then flip the main fuse switch back up again.

In a power cut, check that all appliances are turned off, to avoid the risk of fire should the power supply come on again when you are no longer on the premises.

The water supply in many properties is dependent on a pump bringing water from the underground tanks, so taps should also be turned off so that pumps do not overheat and water supplies are lost.

In the past few years, the increased demand for electricity in Skopelos has caused problems in Skiathos. Plans to run a new line to Skopelos caused residents of Skiathos to organize a protest to stop the project and the matter now is in the hands of the Greek judicial system. Residents of Skopelos are therefore turning more and more to solar energy, at least for their hot water.

With about 2400 hours of sunlight per year Skopelos has the potential to increase its use of solar energy and to develop alternative sources for energy which make use of a frequent and steady northerly wind.

However, at the moment, major construction and mass tourism development projects for hotels and tourist housing have not yet embraced the concept of alternative resources and most recently built projects rely on electricity generated on the mainland, even for hot water.

The power supply on the island is 220v with round 2 pin sockets.

Recycling

Unfortunately, Skopelos lags behind urban Greece in recycling treatment. Until recently, there was no rubbish recycling program on the island. Solid and hazardous waste was deposited in a landfill or dumped unofficially on unattended public or private land.

Periodically families of Roma people come to Skopelos to collect scrap metal from areas around the island where it has been illegally dumped. The scrap metal is removed from the island by lorry and sold on the mainland.

However, the municipal council is now seeking to raise environmental awareness and involvement of the public, and especially young people, in environmental protection and the adoption of simple daily habits like household waste recycling, organic waste composting, energy conservation and 'green' building. It has begun to encourage and undertake activities and initiatives that promote the principles of **ECOWEEK,** which was established on the island of Aegina, Greece in 2005, and is active today in Greece, Cyprus and other countries.

In 2010, Green Week had 'Waste' as its primary theme, and focussed on opportunities for waste minimization, reuse and recycling on the island. The Municipal Council decided to concentrate its attention on large scale waste and its disposal. It has already sent several small containers of electrical appliance waste for recycling to the mainland, and now has a system to collect old appliances (for details, contact the Town Hall +30 24240 22205).

The schools have begun a program on environmental education – concentrating on the use of plastic bags and their recycling.

Small businesses are already involved in battery collection and their safe disposal.

Beer and bulk wine bottles are recycled by the distributors. There is a deposit collected for each bottle at time of purchase which is redeemed upon return.

An understanding of the real cost of waste was complemented by a series of events around the island focusing on its tree and bird life and paths to ensure that **Green Week** goes from strength to strength as an annual event.

However, there remains much still to be done, especially as the major problem is that of expense - one made worse by the recent recession, Greece's financial problems and fuel price increases.

Forest fire as seen from Skopelos Town

Fire!

Skopelos has a small fire-fighting service of between 5 and 8 men. They are supplemented by volunteers, and these are the people to be seen around Skopelos, sitting under the trees in the shade at different vantage points, on fire watch. Volunteers can be male or female, and are unpaid.

Fire watching is the first line of defence on the island, and all the locals are committed to fire prevention as far as possible. In the summer, when the population changes from 5,000 to 30-40,000, the opportunities for carelessness are correspondingly multiplied.

The problem of controlling huge fires is the inaccessible terrain, compounded by a general lack of investment in firefighting equipment and personnel. These areas of concern are intensified by the fact that the Greek government recently prohibited the use helicopters in firefighting for fear that such operations would create additional power cuts (!), a common occurrence in rural Greece.

Because of the terrain, the average response time by fire units serving rural areas is 35 minutes. There is a need for more vehicles offering good off-road performance, manoeuverability, and an ability to climb, with small dimensions and low weight. Unfortunately, this type of vehicle rules out the carrying of large amounts of extinguishing agents.

This year we have had the first heavy rains for the last several years, alleviating a drought. Even though trees with long roots could reach down to the water table and the island retained much of its greenery superficially, the place was actually a tinderbox.

In 2009, Skopelos had to declare a national state of emergency after a major and uncontrolled wildfire that broke out on a Monday ran into its second day. The fire originally broke out in the region of Agnontas, but took on major dimensions due to strong winds blowing overnight, incinerating landscape of great natural beauty. Fortunately, the wind blew from the sea, driving the flames uphill and away from the areas of human habitation.

Local fire-fighters were reinforced by a 12-man forest fire-fighting unit from the town of Volos on the mainland, who were transferred to the island in a Super-Puma all-weather helicopter during the night, while water bombing aircraft and helicopters joined fire-fighting efforts at first light but were hampered by the strong winds blowing in the area.

The fire was burning at three levels. Ground fires burned through soil that is rich in organic matter. Surface fires burned through dead plant material on the ground. And crown fires burned in the tops of shrubs and trees. Only high-intensity fires burn into the crowns of the tallest trees. In this kind of heat pine trees, which are full of resin, can explode like a bomb and the fire is able to jump above the heads of the fire fighters, making the situation extremely dangerous.

The mayor was able to get the situation declared as a state of national emergency, which meant a ferry could be commandeered. By Tuesday morning there was a force of 70 firemen from Thessaly on the ground, while the Air Force General Staff announced that two Canadair CL415 water-bombing aircraft were fighting the flames from the air. These were later augmented by another two aircraft of the same type from Russia, that had been sent to take part in the parade for the March 25 anniversary, and two CL215 aircraft.

The fires were finally brought under control without loss of life, but it was a very worrying time for property owners - some of whom had to use precious water supplies to saturate their houses to prevent them igniting; for the local people, who were all involved in feeding the fire crews and attending to their needs; and for the families of the firemen, who were unable to leave the smouldering areas until they were sure that nothing was going to re-ignite. The burned areas can be seen from the road between Stafilos and Agnontas.

The damaged forests should begin to regenerate in the next few years, but please -

BE CAREFUL WHEN LIGHTING FIRES, OR DISPOSING OF SPENT MATCHES.
KEEP SKOPELOS GREEN ON BLUE!

Transportation

Driving on Skopelos

The best way to see the island of Skopelos is by car or jeep. That way you can get off the beaten track and find deserted coves and beaches, travel without fuss to see the *Mamma Mia!* Church and explore the unspoilt northern part of the island, which is now a national park. You can also control your own pace and, should you fancy a meal or a swim, you can please yourselves. However, please be aware that sign posting is poor and many corners are sharp and not marked.

40 Km of good tarmac road link Skopelos town with Stafilos, Agnontas, Limonari, Panormos and finally Glossa. From Glossa, a road winds down to the port of Loutraki. There is a road from Skopelos Town past the monastery of Ag. Righinos which comes out between Agnontas and Panormos and a road cutting right across the centre of the island from Glossa almost back to Skopelos Town itself.

Secondary roads provide short cuts to various places; they are unmetalled, but perfectly navigable with an ordinary car if one drives slowly and carefully.   There are also many tracks criss-crossing all over the island. Many are in very poor condition, but navigable with 4 wheel drive.

Should you drive on Skopelos, there are several things to remember:

- The use of seatbelts is required by law and is now being strictly enforced.

- Drinking and driving is illegal in Greece, contrary to what you may believe when observing some of the locals! 'Breath-tests' are continually carried out by the local police.

- Surprisingly, considering the amount of noise at the celebration of weddings, christenings, and football matches, it is against the law to use the horn except in an emergency or to avoid a collision.

- If you wish to visit any of the other islands, you will not be permitted to take your hired car with you.

Car Hire

Cars offered for hire on the island are divided into categories according to engine size:

CATEGORY A cars are Hyundai Atos /Kia Picanto

CATEGORY B cars are Renault Clio/Fiat Punto

CATEGORY C cars are Suzuki Jimny jeeps

CATEGORY D cars are Hyundai Accent/Renault Thalia

CATEGORY E cars are Automatic Getz. These are only available on request as there are only 2 Category E cars available on the island.

Prices usually include CDW insurance (with Excess), theft protection, passenger insurance, free delivery and pick up, free mileage and local taxes. The Excess for categories A & B cars is usually 300 euros. For categories C, D & E the Excess is usually 500 euros. Fully Comprehensive insurance can be given at an extra charge.

To hire a car you will need to show your passport and a valid driving licence, which has been held for at least one year. To drive a car, you must be over 23 years old.

You will be given a rental contract, which you should keep in the car to show the police in the event you are stopped. Hire companies will not provide you with log books or separate insurance papers.

Greek law stipulates the use of seat belts and prohibits children under the age of ten from sitting in the front seat of the car. Most car hire companies have child seats.

Should your hire car break down, call the rental company straight away and do not try to move the car; just wait until help arrives.

If you have an accident it is important to keep calm. If there are injuries to yourself or your passengers, call the emergency doctor's number (0030 24240 22222). If possible, call the hire car company too.

Turn off the engine to avoid the risk of fire and move away from the car and out of danger of passing vehicles. If passengers are injured, it is imperative that you do not try to move them.

The car hire company will alert the police, who are obliged to prepare a report of the incident: do not move the car as the police will sketch the position of the vehicles involved in the accident. This is a common practice throughout Europe, so do not allow yourself to be intimidated into moving your car. If the car **has** been moved, any insurance claims will be nullified and you might be asked to pay full costs for repairs, or even replacement.

Scooter /Buggy Hire

As an alternative to 4 wheels, several firms rent mopeds, fully-automatic scooters or low-cc motor bikes. The cost of hire includes third party insurance. It is the law that a helmet must be provided with rented motorbikes.

You may hire a 50cc scooter with a driving licence valid for cars, but for anything more powerful, you will need the correct motorcycle licence. Reputable car/bike hire firms always check your licence.

Many people have a dream of driving with the wind in their hair, whilst acquiring a golden tan quickly on the back of a motorbike. Don't buy into it! Many ungraded roads are covered in loose sand or shale, whilst metalled roads tend to become very greasy after a shower of rain. Sunlight suddenly striking your eyes on hairpin bends can also lead to loss of control. There have been several local deaths in the last few years for reasons such as these.

This is why most agents do not recommend that you hire a bike at all. If you do decide to hire a bike, please wear the helmet provided! And do dress sensibly, sun burn can be just as painful as an accident!

Buggy hire is also not recommended by most holiday companies. They are unstable, and in fact there are very few places where they can be raced, which is what most people want to do!

Mountain Bikes

Skopelos Cycling is a new company on the Stafilos Road, near Terpsis Restaurant. It has Trekking cross 21 speed, Mountain 24 speed and Trekking cross 24 speed bikes for hire. Helmets are included.

Taxi

The taxi rank is at the quayside, next to the harbour and the bus station. The price should be agreed prior with the driver and will vary according to the destination.

You can book a trip and its return with the driver; just tell him what time you wish to be collected and from where. Taxi drivers will give you their mobile phone number and their numbers can also be found in the telephone boxes.

A taxi to Stafilos is approximately 7 euro; to Limnonari approx. 12 euro; to Glossa approx. 25 euro (2009 prices).

Bus

Skopelos is not a large island and during the season transport is good and plentiful. Out of high season, buses run regularly, but not frequently, depending on the demand.

The bus station is at the quayside, next to the harbour and the large parking area. There is no published timetable. Times are written up at the station according to the demands of the season. Tickets are purchased on the bus. It is always wise in low season (May/September) to ask the driver, on disembarkation, when he will return!

Buses go every day from Skopelos Town:

- To Glossa/Loutraki (one hour) *
- To Panormos (25 minutes) *
- To Milia (35 minutes) *
- To Agnontas (15 minutes) *
- To Stafilos (15 minutes) *

* Prices vary between about 1.50 and 4.00 euro (2009 prices) depending on the distance travelled.

Water Taxi

During the season, a regular water taxi departs late morning for Glysteri Beach (in 2009 this was 5 euro, one way), and returns at about 5pm. The boat is to be found along the waterfront by the cafes and restaurants. Times and prices are displayed on a poster by the mooring.

Boat Hire

To further enhance your holiday on the island, you can hire a boat for the day. Imagine cruising leisurely in the crystal clear waters around the coast, and alighting on your own beach 'far from the madding crowd!' Beautiful!

Generally, all boats available for hire on Skopelos were built in the last five years and are equipped with all necessary safety equipment. All have canopies. 15 HP boats can be hired for a maximum of 5 passengers, 30 HP boats for a maximum of 4 passengers. They are licensed by the Port Authority.

Boats can be hired in Skopelos Town from the Madro Travel Office, Thalpos Office (Old Port, Paralea) or from the harbour at Blo. However, sailing is restricted to the lee shore of the island, (which is perfectly safe), as currents around Skopelos town can be treacherous for inexperienced sailors in small boats.

For this reason, the boats are picked up at Blo, Linarakia, or Panormos from 10.00 and must be returned by 19.00 of the last day of hire. Fuel is paid by the client. Full instructions will be given prior to taking the boat out and you will be told where it is permitted to sail. Most beaches are on the lee shore, so restrictions will not spoil your enjoyment of the island.

Boats are insured against third party liability and for material damages in excess of 400 euro according to the   requirements of the Port Authority. Propellors and damages underneath the boat are not covered and damages are paid in full by the client.

Shanks' Pony

Walking on Skopelos usually involves some climbing: if not on the way out, then definitely on the way back! However, the beautiful views will more than make up for the effort involved.

The island has a network of ancient cobbled paths, called Kalderimi, which in the past linked the churches to the springs. You can drink from the springs, or refill your water bottles if you need to, as the water is perfectly safe. There are lots of tracks and paths up in the hills and, apart from areas close to the main road between Skopelos Town and Glossa/Loutraki, you do not find many houses; just some isolated farms and small-holdings. There is quite a network of surfaced roads as well, but these are mostly very narrow and twisting country lanes, often lined by brambles and other vegetation which spill right onto the roads so sometimes it's like going through a tunnel.

Probably the main thing to consider when out walking on Skopelos (especially between June and September) is the heat. If you are off wandering the island **do** take account of the heat - sometimes the weather does not feel as hot as it really is due to the wind. Even on a cloudy day it is possible to be badly burned, if you do not have adequate protection.

Remember to take plenty of water and a hat.

There are no established walks with directional signposts, distances and times marked. Walkers can use the **Road Edition map** which is quite accurate as far as tracks and country lanes are concerned but does not have all footpaths marked. Alternatively, there is the excellent **TOPO** hiking map of Skopelos from **Anavasi**. This relief map has paths and tracks and is gps friendly, so getting lost is not an issue. In fact with the quality of these maps, making up and then doing particular walks is straightforward. You can buy the map at Madro Travel, Old Port, Paralea – price at this time is 6 euro.

Panormos beach - family resort with tavernas

Accommodation

There are many rooms, apartments, hotels and villas available on Skopelos. Prices are lowest off season – May and end of September/October- and highest in the peak season of July and August, when many Greeks come from Athens and the mainland for their holidays.

One or two landlords meet the ferries coming in, but this is not encouraged and they have to wait outside the port gate. A better option is the Rent Rooms association of Skopelos, which has a small office opposite the port entrance. The staff here will try to find you accommodation at a price to match your budget.

However, during peak season accommodation is at a premium and it is possibly foolhardy to try to find accommodation on arrival in this period. Far better to use one of the various holiday companies (Sunvil Holidays, Greek Islands Club, Thalpos Holidays, Ionian Holidays, Aegean Island Holidays, Thomson Holidays, Thomas Cook and Olympic Holidays) offering a complete package of flight, accommodation and transfers; or, if you wish to travel independently, trust to the offices of Madro Travel and Dolphin. You might like to check out their websites that are listed in the 'useful contacts' chapter of this book.

Out of season (mid-October to the end of April) there is limited hotel accommodation available and the majority of apartments and studios are closed – they are not geared up for off-season occupation.

Please note that there are no official camp sites on Skopelos.

The hotels and pensions here by no means represent all the accommodation available on Skopelos. All accommodations are in alphabetical order with the aim of providing a range to suit all budgets. Please check skopelos.web/skopelos.net/madrotravel.com and 'useful contacts' for further information.

Skopelos Town

Aeolos Hotel 3 star: +30 24240 22233/+30 24240 23233
email: aeolosae@otenet.gr

Agnanti Hotel 2 star: +30 24240 22722 email: massaras@otenet.gr

Amalia Hotel 2 star: +30 24240 22688 email: amaliag@otenet.gr

Aperitton 3 star: +30 24240 22256 email: aperitton@otenet.gr

Del Sol Apartments: +3024240 23334 email: delsol@otenet.gr

Dionyssos Hotel 3 star: +30 24240 23210 email: info@dionyssoshotel.com

Dolphin Hotel 3 star: +30 24240 23017

Denise Hotel: +30 24240 22678

Elli Hotel 2 star: +30 24240 22943

Georgios L. Hotel 1 star: +30 24240 23355 / 23010 / 22308
email : georgios-hotel@skopelos.net

Ionia 3 star: +30 24240 22568 e mail: hotelionia@vol.forthnet.gr

Kyria Sotos Pension: +30 24240 22549/30 24240 22808 (All year availability)
email : sotossko@otenet.gr

Lina Guest House B&B: +30 24240 23976

Prince Stafilos: +30 24240 22775

Rigas Hotel: +30 24240 22618

Skopelos Village Suite Hotel 4 star: +30 24240 22517
email: info@skopelosvillage.gr

Sun Pension 3 keys: +30 24240 23784 email: sun@skopelos.net

Sunrise Village Hotel 2 star: +30 24240 23002/+30 24240 23533
email: sunrise@skopelos.net

Villa Ble Apartments: +30 24240 23350

Stafilos
Alkistis Apartment Hotel 4 star: +30 24240 22117
email: alkistis@skopeloshotels.com

Ariadne Stafilos : +30 24240 22772

Ostria Hotel Stafilos 2 star: +30 24240 22220/30 24240 23236
email: ostria20@otenet.gr

Pegasus Apartments: +30 24240 22 671/ 24 411

Pelagos Apartments: +30 24240 22818 email: arhipelagos@skopelos.travel

Panagiotas Studios : + 30 24240 22604

Skopelos Holidays Hotel and Spa 4 star: +30 24240 24302
email : skophol@otenet.gr

The Two Brothers Studio/Apartments: +30 24240 22576 / +30 24240 22403

Agnontas

Apartments Althea: +30 24240 22589

Lithanemon Apartments: +30 24240 22512

Panormos and Milia Beach

Adrina Beach Hotel 5 star (from end of 2010): +30 24240 23373-5
email: info@adrina.gr

Adrina Beach Hotel 4 star: +30 24240 23373-5 email: info@adrina.gr

Afrodite Hotel: +30 24240 23622 email: info@afroditehotel.gr

Milia Studios Milia Beach: +30 24240 23 998/+30 24240 22 735

Spirou Blue Suites Panormos: +30 24240 22142

Elios

Apartments Dia: +30 24240 33 311/+30 6932099575

Delphi studios and apartments: +30 24240 33301

Hovolo Apartments: +30 24240 33151

Zaneta Apartments: +30 24240 33140

Glossa and Loutraki

Apartments Violetta: +30 24240 33474/+30 24240 33043

Evagelia studios: +30 24240 33831 / +30 24240 33065

Rania studios: +30 24240 33710

Selenunda Hotel (Glossa Loutraki) : +30 24240 34073/ +30 24240 33570

Faros Studios (Loutraki): +30 24240 33100

Ninemia (Loutraki): +30 24240 33728

For rooms to let, check out www.skopelosweb.gr and www.skopelosnet.gr.

For villas with pools out of town, as well as a variety of apartments and studios, check out Madro Travel and Thalpos websites.

A new venture in accommodation for Skopelos is Appaloosa Valley Yurts, situated about 5km from Skopelos town.

Tel: +30 69895 28290 www.appeloosavalleyyurts-skopelos.com

The hillside village of Glossa

Eating Out

Greeks love eating! Their main meal tends to be dinner at the end of the day, and we mean the end of the day, as Greeks like to eat late. The evening meal with Greeks is very much a social occasion and can happen any time from 2100 hrs to Midnight!

Lunch is normally served in tavernas from midday until about 1400hrs, sometimes later. The Greeks are happy to oblige and it seems that if you are hungry they are quite happy to feed you!

If you find it difficult understanding the Greek menu, do not worry- it is still customary in many places in Skopelos to go into the kitchen area and see what has been prepared as a first hand reference of what is available. Of course, due to the long arm of EC regulations, these dishes are now behind glass.

On Skopelos, if you are with a group of friends and you wish to go out to eat, you do not ask '**Where** shall we eat?', but rather '**What** shall we eat?' This will decide where you are going!

Places to eat fall into different categories:

The **Taverna** tends to be a place where people go for a night out, usually with a group of friends. It may have a limited range of main dishes, but quite a lot of starters (Mezzes). A taverna may not even have a menu so the waiter will recite a list of what is available, or you may be invited into the kitchen to see what takes your fancy. Akrotiri around the bay towards Palouki is an example of the most traditional kind of taverna.

The **Estiatorio** is usually open all day and is particularly busy at lunchtimes. Most of the baked dishes are pre-cooked in large containers, so you should get quick service. It is here that you find the most traditional dishes involving long, slow cooking and maximum preparation. Examples of these are Ta Kimata, O Molos and Klimataria at the Old Port, Paralea, Skopelos Town. These are traditional in that, like most Greeks, you order for the table, **not** for individuals and you share the dishes. Of course you can order a dish for yourself, but you will tend to have to order salad and potatoes separately. Ask what comes with the dish. Most estiatoria serve take-away meals.

The **Psarotaverna** is a taverna specializing in fish and seafood. There are no exclusively Psarotavernas in Skopelos Town as fresh fish is readily available, but Ta Kimata has its own small fishing boats and O Molos and Klimataria are situated directly opposite where the fishing boats tie up in Skopelos: Korali and Pavlos psarotavernas are on the beach in Agnontas and Flisvos is situated along the beach to the right of the port in Loutraki.

The **Psistaria (ΨΙΣΤΕΡΙΑ)** is a taverna that serves only grilled meats. Peparithos on the ring road of Skopelos Town calls itself a psistaria, but has other more traditional dishes on the menu as well. Spitalia around the bay towards Palouki is a true psistaria.

An **Ouzery** specialises in mezedes, but has a very small menu for main meals. Examples of these are Yialos on the Paralea; Karidia on the ring road to the right of the T junction; and Gorgonas in the town opposite the church of Nikolaos. There is also the Anatoli on top of the Kastro, owned by Giorgos Xintaris, which on occasion has live rembetika music (NB. music does not begin until 22.00). Apolavsi is a family run establishment, cheap and cheerful, on the road to the T junction opposite the car hire places in Skopelos town. There is also a new ouzery 'O Oraia Ellas' (splendid Greece) just opened in Loutraki opposite the play park.

Greek restaurants do not really serve deserts, usually only fresh fruit. It is also not a Greek habit to drink coffee after a meal, so coffee may not always be available. Those looking for something sweet go to a Zacharoplasteio after a meal.

A **Zacharoplasteio** is a place where people meet to chat over coffee, tea and soft drinks. It is also where you can find a selection of Pasta (cakes) or Pagato (ice cream). Nowadays, many of these places refer to themselves merely as Cafes. Alcoholic drinks are also served. Korali, Karavia, Gala and Skopelos Zacharoplasteio are on the Paralea in Skopelos Town; Kyr. Eleni is on the right just before the main square in Glossa; and Korali and Cafe Aramis are at the harbour of Loutraki, opposite the play park.

A **Kafeneion** is also a place to drink coffee. It is traditionally a place where the men gather to play cards or Tavli (Backgammon), read their newspapers or simply to talk; solving the latest political crisis or clinching a new business deal, or just whiling away the time in peaceful meditation with their Komboloi (worry beads). A cup of coffee may last for hours! Look for them in the towns and villages. The one in Skopelos Town is on the Paralea and is a Public Kafeneion. This means that it is subsidised by the council to provide cheaper refreshment for older citizens.

Snackbars sell a range of sandwiches, plain or toasted and a selection of savoury pies. These are made with filo pastry and the fillings are usually spinach (spinakopitta), cheese (tyropitta), sausage (loukanopitta), wild greens (hortopitta). The International Cafe, En Plo and Barremares are examples of these on the Paralea in Skopelos town, but there are many more. Bakeries also sell a selection of sandwiches and drinks to take away.

Fast Food – Pizzas/Gyros/Souvlaki

These are mostly situated in the square directly opposite the port behind the bakery and in the area around the newsagents in Skopelos Town. La Tana pizza house is on the ring road and delivers. Pizza is sold by the metre at Pizza A La Metro on the Paralea.

Pies/Puddings and Cakes

All the bakeries, especially the Kochylis Bakery opposite the port, sell pies, but for home-baked chicken pies, quiche (sold by the slice) sponge cakes and rice puddings, go to Iliopita on the way to the post office, opposite the open air cinema.

Tourist Tavernas abound. They serve **merides** (plated meals of the kind found in all European restaurants, with meat or fish etc accompanied on the same plate by potatoes, vegetables or salad) and have full menus. Examples of these are Englezos, Nostos and Alexander's.

Restaurants serve a mixture of European–type dishes with some traditional elements. Wine is usually only served by the bottle, which can make meals a little more expensive. Examples of these in Skopelos Town are Anna's Restaurant (live music at the weekend), follow the signs up the high street; Perivoli through Platanos Square behind the bakery opposite the port; To Rodi, follow the high street and it is on the right, just before Alexander's; Alexander's itself; Finikas, and Agioli (in Skopelos Village hotel) round the bay; Terpsis in Stafilos whose speciality is chicken stuffed with liver, walnuts and prunes (you will need to order this the day before; ring +30 24240 22053); and Agnanti Restaurant in Glossa.

Nastas, by the T junction in Skopelos Town (with the blue boat outside) is all things to all men – psarotaverna, psistaria, ouzeri, estiatorio and restaurant, but whatever you eat, it's good. Keep an eye out through the season as they are licensed to provide live music on special occasions.

Bakeries and Pie Shops

There are several bakeries in Skopelos Town, one in Elios and one in Glossa. Kyr. Eleni, round the building where the newsagency is situated in Skopelos Town, makes and sells traditional breads, cakes and sweets.

Traditional Sweets

Kyr. Eleni in Skopelos Town and Glossa (already mentioned under bakeries); Ambrosia on the Paralea; and Alexandras on the street above the old OTE about 100 metres on the right all sell walnut stuffed chocolate covered plums, as well as other delicious homemade sweets.

Hungry? Now for the real food!

Traditional estiatoria restaurants, Old Port, Paralea, Skopelos Town

'Mezedes'

The Greek cuisine is rich in Mezedes, from olives to fried and baked cheeses, to more complicated dishes such as dolmades (stuffed vine leaves) or stuffed peppers and tomatoes. Be careful, it is very easy to overdo the Mezedes, and find it difficult to eat your main course. This has been known to happen on many an occasion!

Horiatiki Salad is the traditional Greek Salad, consisting of sliced tomatoes, cucumber, onions, green peppers and feta cheese sprinkled with oregano (Greeks have oregano with everything!) and soaked in olive oil. This can be eaten as a starter or with the main dish.

Feta Cheese is usually served along with the salad as a starter but may also be eaten with the main dish. It will be sprinkled with oregano and oil. When ordering, if you prefer it without oil, ask for it 'horis ladhee'. A delicious way to eat feta is baked in the oven. If you wish to try this ask for 'feta fourno'. Feta is made from sheep or cow's milk and is pure white and very creamy.

Taramasalata is the roe of either grey mullet or cod blended with breadcrumbs, olive oil, lemon juice and onions made into a fine paste which is pink and is eaten as a bread dip.

Tzatziki is a dip made from yoghurt with garlic, cucumber and parsley. A very refreshing starter.

Scorthalia is made with mashed potatoes, garlic and oil. This dish is usually eaten with cod fish in batter, usually cold. Beware, it is very garlicky!

Kolokethakia are fried courgettes or marrows.

Meletzanes are sliced aubergines fried in oil.

Vegetarian Dishes

Not many tavernas or restaurants label their dishes as vegetarian, but that does not mean that this need is not catered for. The one place you must avoid if you are vegetarian, is the psistaria, which caters primarily for the carnivore!

Greece has many traditional vegetarian dishes, including:

Gigantes (giant beans in a tomato sauce)

Revithia (chickpeas baked in soups or fritters)

Ratatouille-type dishes such as **Briam** and **Imam**, and a variety of **Keftedes** (vegetable fritters)

Gemista (tomatoes and peppers stuffed with rice and herbs)

Horta (wild greens served with lemon and oil)

Spinaki (Plate of spinach in lemon and oil)

Dolmades (Vine leaves stuffed with rice and herbs)

Horiatiki (Greek salad - tomatoes, cucumber, olives & onions, topped with feta cheese, sprinkled with oregano and drizzled with olive oil)

Saganaki (Fried cheese)

Spinakopitta (spinach pie)

Dips, in the salad list of the menu, such as

Tzatziki (cucumber, yoghurt & garlic)

Skordalia (potato & garlic)

Melitzanosalata (aubergine)

Now - the main courses!

On the grill

Brizola (pork chop)
Paithakia (lamb chops)
Souvlaki (pork, swordfish or chicken grilled on a skewer)
Loukaniko (sausage)
Sikoti (liver)
Kotopoulo fileto (chicken fillet)
Moshari (veal) on a Greek menu simply means younger beef
Katsiki (goat) is often described on menus as 'special lamb' and is well worth trying
Biftekia (Something akin to hamburgers)

Sto Forno (from the oven)

Arni (lamb)

Kotopoulo (chicken)

Keftedes (Small meatballs)

Souzoukakia (small meatballs cooked in tomato sauce)

Stifado are stews and tend to be very tasty, whether shrimp, pork, beef, rabbit or lamb - cooked with tomato and little onions

Fish

Fish is priced and bought by the kilo in tavernas, so don't have a heart attack when you see the menu! But fish is not cheap, so you may prefer to have fish as part of mezedes, when the portions are smaller and priced as a plate. Should you want fish as a main dish, you can usually select your own and then check the weight and agree the price. It is then cooked on a charcoal grill in the kitchen.

A selection to choose from is as follows:

Barbouni	Red mullet
Lithrini	Bream
Garides	Prawns
Ksifia	Swordfish
Kalamari	Squid
Oktopothi	Octopus
Astakos	Lobster
Marides	Small fish
Gavros	Whitebait
Bakaliar	Hake or cod, fried (as a fillet, this is the nearest thing to English fish and chips!)
Tonnos	Tuna
Xtapothi	Octopus

Main Dishes

Soups are often made from fish with either fresh tomatoes or eggs and lemon juice. Best served chilled, these soups are mostly found in fish restaurants.

Tiropitta is a light tasty snack made with filo pastry and filled with cream cheese or feta. Tiropittas are baked fresh each morning and are best when still piping hot from the oven. Also served in small triangles as a starter, but called **bourokakia** in this case.

Moussaka is perhaps the most popular Greek dish found in most tavernas. However as with everything, fresh is best. It is made with minced beef or lamb, aubergines, potatoes and topped with a béchamel sauce and a little grated cheese.

Souvlaki is served just about everywhere and consists of charcoal-grilled pieces of pork, beef or chicken on a skewer with green peppers, tomatoes and onions. It may sometimes be served on its own with lemon juice and oregano.

Yemistes are large tomatoes or green peppers stuffed with rice, vegetables and sometimes minced meat or feta. If you do not want minced meat, say 'horis kreeas'.

Gouvetsi is a traditional Greek dish cooked in a round shallow earthenware casserole called a gouvetsi. It consists of lamb cooked in a tomato sauce with macaroni or 'hilopites' (noodles).

Dolmathes are made with vine leaves stuffed with rice and sautéed with olive oil and herbs. There are many variations on this dish and it may be eaten hot or cold and sometimes served with a lemon flavoured béchamel sauce.

Pastitsio is a dish of macaroni baked with layers of cheese and minced meat.

Keftethes are cooked meatballs with herbs; usually they come in a red tomato and olive oil sauce.

Rabbit is a delicacy. It is cooked in a special spicy tomato sauce, a **stifado**. A delicious dish, and very popular with the locals.

Seafood is best eaten in the special fish restaurants. Grey mullet is delicious when marinated in lemon juice, olive oil and oregano and then charcoal grilled.

Astakos is lobster, and can be found in all good fish restaurants. At Nastas in Skopelos Town and Korali at Agnontas, you can choose your own from the tanks.

Fish is always served complete with the head, the best part according to the locals.

Kalamari is squid, deep-fried or grilled on charcoal and sprinkled with lemon juice.

Cheese and Fruit

Whilst you are on Skopelos you may want to cook or make up a picnic. Most supermarkets have a delicatessen counter, where you can buy olives, cooked meats and cheese. Do not expect Sainsbury's!

You may be unfamiliar with the following cheeses:

Kefalotiri	A hard slightly bitter cheese good for frying as it goes soft but does not spread all over the pan. It is also suitable for grating over pasta.
Graviera	Very similar to the above.
Feta	A soft creamy cheese, often served on a 'Greek' salad.
Mizithra	A soft white creamy cheese.
Manouri	A white semi-soft cheese.
Regato	A hard full-flavoured yellow cheese, resembling mild Cheddar.

Bread - olive bread, cheese bread, traditional bread and pies can be supplied by the bakeries.

Fruit

Melon and watermelon can be bought very cheaply. In general, as the Greeks eat large quantities of fruit, the greengrocers are used to selling their products by the carrier bag full. The fruit market is in the same building as the Amalia Hotel on the road to the T junction. There is a good selection further down the same road outside the supermarkets. Look out for locals selling fruit from their gardens - they will put a sign on their gate.

Be aware that in hot weather, as few agricultural chemicals are used, fruit & vegetables will perish more quickly than we are used to in UK.

Sweetmeats, coffee and cakes

Sweetmeats

Although many locals have a sweet tooth, desserts are not normally offered after a meal. Instead a cake or a pastry is eaten in the afternoon with a Greek coffee. Pastries are very sweet and oozing with honey or syrup and usually nuts.

Some of the better known are;

Baclavas - the best known sweet, made with filo pastry, honey and almonds.

Galactobouriko - baked milk pudding topped with filo pastry, syrup and cinnamon (Milk Pie).

Kataifi - walnuts, cinnamon and honey in a shredded pastry.

Other sweets :

Rizogolo - almost an English rice pudding- normally served cold.

Yiorti - Yoghurt

Meli - Honey

Milopita - Apple pie

Halva - There are two types, either made with semolina and sold in slices like a cake, or made with sesame seeds. Various flavours are available from shops. This is the only sweet the Orthodox are allowed to eat in Lent.

Ordering coffee

Coffees are many and various - from Frappe (iced coffee), to Nes (instant coffee), to Greek coffee. **Elleniko Kafe** is the traditional Greek coffee (*not* to be called Turkish coffee), which is served in a small cup and is very black, strong and an intense dose of caffeine. Should you want Greek coffee it is important to say how sweet you want it. The sugar is added to the **'Briki'** (the long handled coffee pot that it is heated in) before boiling.

Medium sweet   **Metrio**

Very sweet   **Glyko**

Without sugar   **Sketo**

Tsai is tea, generally served with a sachet of sugar. Remember to ask for lemon or milk.

Wines and Spirits of Greece

Retsina

In a taverna, the choice of wine will probably be limited. Many serve the country's best-known wine, retsina, with its distinctive pine resin taste so admirably suited to Greek food - in fact, you may acquire a taste for it. The ancient Greeks stored their wine in clay *amphorae* sealed with resin; the disintegration of the resin helped prevent oxidation and lent the wine a flavour that caught on (and is now supplied by pieces of resin). Traditionally retsina comes in chilled copper-anodized cans, by the kilo (about a litre), *misokilo* (half) *tetarto* (250ml) and is served in tumblers. Kourtaki is a reliable bottled variety and widely available, but Malamatina is often claimed to be the best. The colour of retsina is important - it should be pale: Retsina becomes darker in colour and much more like a bad sherry as it ages. Some older Greeks like this, but most people do not.

Wine from the barrel

These days, most **house wines** *(krasi chima)* are unresinated and can be incredibly good, but there are still some stinkers around, so start with just a *tetarto* when you order. In summer, the reds often come as chilled as the whites. When drinking in Greece, 'yamas' is the equivalent of 'cheers'.

Bottled wine

Naoussa: the best known red wine of Macedonia, cultivated from the Xynomavro grapes grown around Mt. Vermio at 1,150ft, where winters are cold and summers are hot.

Rapsani: dry red wines from Xynomavro, Krasato and Stavroto varietals, grown on the lower slopes of Mt. Olympus, where winters are cold and wet and summers very hot.

Anchialos: a soft fruity white wine from Rhoditis and Savatiano grapes, grown by the Pagasitic Gulf in Thessaly. Savatiano has long been used for retsina.

Nemea: the great noble dry red wine of the Peloponnese, cultivated southeast of Corinth from the local Agiorgitiko grapes.

Patras: the hills around Patras are one of southern Greece's top wine growing areas. Rhoditis is used to produce dry whites, while Mavrodaphne, blended with Korinthiaki, is aged to produce velvety Mavrodaphne, one of Greece's great dessert wines, similar to port.

Kefalonia: celebrated bone-dry white Robolo. From a very low yielding grape grown only on the Ionians. Kefalonia also produces sweet red wine, related to Mavrodaphne.

Samos: a dry Muscat cultivated on steep vineyards, terraced from sea level. This white dessert wine, with its apricot nuances, is one of Greece's finest.

Santorini: whipped by winds, with little rainfall, volcanic Santorini produces very distinct dry white wines from Assyrtiko, one of Greece's best white grapes, blended with Athiri and Aedani, resulting in fruity, crispy or even slightly smoky wines.

Rhodes: fragrant lemony whites from Athiri grapes and reds exclusively from the ancient black grape Mandelaria, grown on the northern slopes of Mt Attaviros.

Spirits

Metaxa Brandy

Metaxa is a Greek distilled spirit invented by Spyros Metaxas, from the island of Kefalonia. In 1888, a little over 50 years after the Greek War of Independence, as a young, enthusiastic, businessman he thought that his taverna was not good enough. He wanted more elegance, more challenges.

He created the first Greek brandy and was involved in the foundation of the first distillation facility. He visualized a drink that would conquer the world and therefore he soon built new factories in Constantinople (present-day Istanbul) and in Odessa.

In 1900 the first exports to the United States took place and the brandy became known as the flying brandy. Metaxa is the only Greek industry that survived the two world wars. In 1968 the factory was rebuilt and, although it now consists of state-of-the-art equipment, its output tastes the same as from the traditional method. Metaxa won over the toughest critics and has earned a respected position in the pantheon of fine spirits. In 1989 the company was bought by the British drinks group Grand Metropolitan (now re branded as Diageo) and was later sold to the Remy Cointreau group.

The label shows a Salaminomaho (Salamina fighter), a figure of an Ancient Greek fighter that was carved on a coin of that era and found during the excavation of the first factory in 1888.

Metaxa is a blend of brandy and wine made from sun-dried Savatiano, Sultana and Black Corinth grape varieties. It is then blended with an aged Muscat wine from the Greek islands of Samos and Lemnos. It is exported to over 60 countries. It comes in five major varieties: Three Stars, Five Stars, Seven Stars, Twelve Stars and the Grand Reserve. The number of stars represents the number of years the blend is matured. The three and 5 star are not very different, except that the 5 star is notably drier, making the alcohol more pronounced. The seven and twelve star are more flavoursome and complex, while the twelve is again more dry, in this case because there is no addition of wine. In either of the two latter varieties, the smell and taste of the barrel in which the brandy matured is noticeable. The Grand Reserve is the most expensive and difficult to find. Aficionados prefer the 5 star.

The Twelve-Star version is now distributed internationally. Additional varieties and collectors' items, such as the Grand Olympian Reserve Celebration Edition, are available only in some regions.

Metaxa is traditionally served neat, on the rocks, or mixed (usually with sours).

Ouzo - The Greek Spirit

Greeks are usually a calm(!) and happy people and have a special way of enjoying life. They don't drink to get drunk. They consider drinking as a way of relaxing and socializing, and a chance to get together and drinking ouzo is an art form.

Ouzo, the 'national drink' of Greece, reflects the traditional and the modern Greek way of life, the casual and light attitude of the Greek people and is the spokesman of what the Greeks call 'kefi' (happy and joyful mood). It can be enjoyed everywhere: on a veranda overlooking the Aegean Sea, with friends at home or in specialized restaurants called 'Ouzeries' (a type of Greek taverna, serving a lot of small, different dishes - 'meze' - usually seafood, and serving almost exclusively ouzo. A place to relax, enjoy a good conversation with friends, eat, drink ouzo and be happy!) Ouzeries are small traditional restaurants; warm, friendly and cosy.

They serve, of course, ouzo and a large variety of foods in small portions, the well-known 'mezedes' (plural for 'meze'). The mezedes, as a concept, resemble the Spanish concept of 'tapas', i.e. small portions of many different tastes. Ouzo is best enjoyed when combined with mezedes, such as grilled octopus, fried or grilled calamari, various other seafood, dried mackerel, 'sardeles pastes' (salted sardines), 'koukia' (broad beans), olives, feta cheese, cucumber, tomatoes, salty food etc. Mezedes keep the effects of the strong alcohol from overwhelming you and enable you to enjoy your ouzo slowly, for hours, in a profoundly calm state of mind where all is beautiful and life is great! In the villages, where life is 'slow', ouzo is enjoyed during the day, with lunch, or a snack, or during the night, with dinner.

There are three ways in which we enjoy ouzo: 'Straight', taking small sips in order to get the true flavour of the spirit (if you are a first time Ouzo drinker, we suggest that you don't drink it straight!); slightly diluted with cold water for a smoother taste; or 'on the rocks' for a cooler, more aromatic taste (you can also add water to dilute even further). Remember that Ouzo is drunk with 'respect', in small, slow sips, so that it can 'compose' its taste.

You will notice that the crystal clear ouzo liquid becomes opaque and 'cloudy' when combined with water. This occurs because the anise oil that is contained in ouzo dissolves and becomes 'invisible' when contained in the conventional alcohol content (38-42% Alcohol/Volume). As soon as the alcohol content is reduced by adding water or ice, the essential oils transform into white crystals, thus making the liquid magically transform into a white, cloudy colour. The same phenomenon occurs when ouzo is stored in a refrigerator. However, in this case ouzo resumes its former state as soon as it is placed at room temperature.

And finally:

Tsipouro - The ancestor of Ouzo

Now you can know what the Greeks know - tsipouro is the insider drink of choice in the tavernas in the mountain villages of Northern Greece and the island of Skopleos. A cousin to ouzo, tsipouro, which does not share its same strong anise flavouring, has been a closely guarded secret until recently - mainly because until the eighties it was illegal to distill Tsipouro except for home consumption. Some tavernas still brew the drink according to their own recipe and the addition of herbs and spices means that many different flavours are to be found among tsipouro varieties. Try it straight, over ice, or with water, accompanied by appetizers.

The locals often ask for tsipouro as a meal at lunchtime. But, if you wish to follow suit, beware. Tsipouro is not drunk with meat, only with fish, sea food, or vegetables and salad. And you cannot choose the food that you want to eat. You ask for tsipouro by the small bottle and the dishes arrive. The food which is served is at the discretion of the cooks, who pride themselves on not serving any of the same food twice within a meal.

Tsipouro is not listed as a meal on the menu. Say 'Tsipouro' and the number of people. As you come to the end of a course, order another round. You should also drink plenty of water. 4 tsipouro per person will give you great food and plenty to eat. For the best tsipouro meal, it is better to go as a foursome, as you get a better variety of dishes.

Tsipouro meals are the cheapest way to eat on the islands.

Warning! There is no point in having tsipouro as a meal if you don't have plenty of time.

Convivial charm

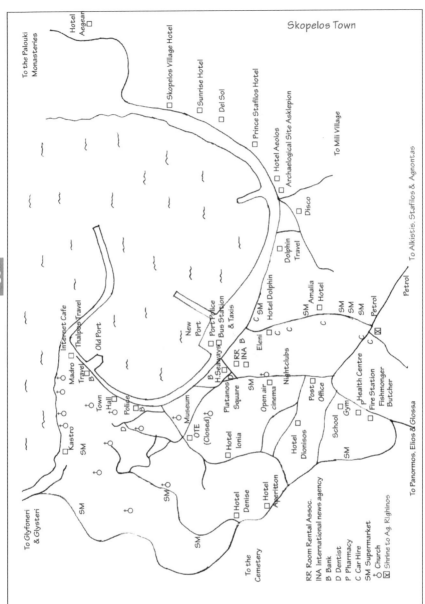

Skopelos Town Map

Shopping

Skopelos

Along the waterfront area – the Paralea - are tourist boutiques/shops selling everything the holidaymaker may require, from suntan lotion to beachwear. There is also a jeweller's shop which makes its own original designs.

Away from the front, you will find shops, supermarkets, bakeries, butchers, cake shops/cafes, stationers, pharmacies, local Greek fast-food/take away places, pizza places, numerous restaurants/tavernas and nightclubs playing a selection of Greek and popular music. There is an internet café situated at the far end of the old harbour.

The high street proper splits into two and has a roughly horseshoe shape, beginning and ending at the harbour front. Here you will find a variety of specialist gift shops, jewellers, clothes' shops, electrical shops, a launderette and shops selling household goods.

It is worth exploring the old back streets up to the Kastro, as you may come across a little gem of a shop you might otherwise have missed. Try the locally produced Skopelos honey, traditionally eaten with fresh local rich creamy yoghurt found in the supermarkets.

Traditional Workshops in Skopelos Town

There are still many craftsmen on the island, producing arts and crafts according to traditional methods. The following all have workshops that can be visited.

Violeta Sofikitou Folklore Pottery Skopelos Town. Violetta is of Russian descent and paints on china and glass. Tel: +30 24240 22148

Christos Patsis Knife Making Skopelos Town, found through Lichnos' shop. Tel: +30 24240 22574

Chromata Skopelou Ceramic Workshop up the hill, opposite Rodi Restaurant Skopelos Town. Elizabeth makes pottery with handpainted designs inspired by the colours of Skopelos. Orders upon request. Tel: +30 69368 85998

Armoloi Pottery Created in 1979 by ceramic artists Nikos Markou and Eleni Lambrous. They work with clay, colour and glazes to create beautiful, decorative and useful ceramics inspired by nature and Greek traditions. Tel: +30 24240 22028

Anthi Valsamaki Icon Painting. An archivist at the Benaki Museum in Athens, Anthi gives occasional workshops on the history and painting of icons. Tel: +30 24240 23106

Alexandra Lace and Textiles high street Skopelos Town. Alexandra provides an outlet for lace and textiles produced by the ladies of the island. Tel: +30 24240 22768

Eleftherios Giannakopoulos Handmade Jewellery and workshop situated on the harbour front, Skopelos Town. This shop has its own handmade pieces, mainly in gold and precious stones. See them at work in their workshop. Tel: +30 24240 22705

Archipelagos, also on the harbour front, sponsors Greek artists throughout the country and provides an outlet for their work. Tel: +30 24240 23127

Rodios Pottery Workshop opposite their shop on the main harbour road. The Rodios family have passed their pottery skills from generation to generation, receiving 10 gold prizes and being honoured with the Athens Academy prize for their pottery patents. Tel: +30 24240 23605

Stafilos

Skopelos has two large supermarkets situated on the Stafilos road, between a half kilometre and two kilometres out of town. The first is **Marinopoulos**, part of the Carrefore chain, which opened in 2010. The second is **Dia**, a discount supermarket offering everything from food and drink to household goods. A third large supermarket is due to open in the summer of 2010 opposite the Amalia Hotel, close to the port in Skopelos Town.

In the season, many small supermarkets spring up along the Stafilos road, catering for all needs from bread, fruit, and groceries to surfboards and plastic sandals.

Agnontas

There is a mini market and a small tourist kiosk in the summer – nothing out of season.

Panormos

There are several lively tavernas along the Panormos shore offering ranks of sun beds. There are also a few shops and a couple of mini markets to serve the growing numbers of hotels and apartments that have sprung up in the area, operating only in the season.

Elios

There are plenty of mini-markets in Elios as well as shops selling the usual tourist fare, a butcher and a bakery. There are also several good tavernas near the new marina for you to spend a relaxing few hours.

Glossa

Although only a small town, Glossa has bakeries, butchers, and a couple of supermarkets/mini-markets. These obviously cater for the local population, so therefore may not contain the full range of goods that you may be used to. Kyra Eleni bakery, just before you reach the town centre on the corner, is considered by many to be the best on the island. She has traditional breads and sweets, as well as local nuts and honey. There is a bank, a couple of cafes and a few specialist/tourist shops, as well as an excellent restaurant. Be aware that many shops keep what may seem to be irregular hours, and may close in the afternoon from approximately 13:00 - 17:00, for siesta. Main shopping requirements will probably have to be met in Skopelos Town.

Loutraki

There are many cafes and restaurants in the village and two fish tavernas, as well as a butcher and a bakery. Again, main shopping requirements will probably have to be met in Skopelos Town.

Monument to sailors and fishermen, Skopelos Old Port Paralea

Nightlife

This is a low key affair: for many tourists, evenings are spent wining and dining in small restaurants and tavernas.

There are many bars on the island, not just in Skopelos Town but also in Glossa on the road to Loutraki and in Loutraki itself. In Elios, bars spring up in the season. Skopelos is not a place for partying every day and every night, but there is quite a good nightlife in a jazzy, sophisticated way.

In Skopelos Town, most of the places are very small and can be found both at the harbour and in the little winding streets. In the evening, the town becomes lively with its many taverns and little bars everywhere. The shops stay open until late, and the atmosphere is convivial.

Night Clubs

The night clubs in Skopelos Town are situated on the same street as the post office and are traditionally Greek, with disco and live music and dancing, but may play foreign music also. They open from about 23:00 onwards and people dance until the small hours, or until dawn. Don't worry, they are soundproofed and air-conditioned.

In **Skopelos**: Ammos; Raise: on the road to the post office. In **Glossa/ Loutraki**: Kivotos: on the road down to Loutraki.

Bar Billiards/Snooker

In Skopelos Town: The Owl Bar on the road to the T junction.

Bouzoukia

In **Skopelos**: Thalasies Chandres is on the road to the Post Office, next to Ammos. A bouzoukia plays traditional Greek music, most people sit at tables and you can throw flowers at the artistes (the modern equivalent of smashing plates.)

Bars

Skopelos Town: Pablos (a wine bar with a lovely view from its balconies and roof terrace over the harbour) situated over Ta Kimita and Platanos (a bar that is great for breakfast) at the old port; Anemos, La Costa, Bardon, Dokos on the paralea; The Blue Bar in town, opposite the church of Ag, Nikolaos and up the steps; Mercurios , above the Adonis Hotel; Mythos Bar, Karavi (in the hull of a sailing ship on dry land, only open in high season) and Karyatis (also only open in high season) around the bay on the way to Palouki; The Garden Bar near the post office.

Agnontas: Korali Cafe Bar on the beach.

Milia: Beach bar in high season.

Glossa/Loutraki: Barka, down on the front at the port.

This is not an exhaustive list, obviously. Explore and find your own favourite.

Music on Skopelos

The typical music style on Skopelos is called 'Rebétiko' or 'Rembetika', and its roots are found in the Greek music of the middle 19th century on the West coast of Asia Minor and Constantinople. It developed in the underworld of Greek cities like Athens or Siros, after the catastrophe in Asia Minor and the expelling of the Greeks from these places resulted in the concentration of people in areas ill-equipped to provide homes or jobs. The name of this music style has to do with the under-privileged of the diaspora, many of whom had little choice but to become part of the underworld of petty crime and drug taking. Rembetika itself refers to those 'low-class men living in the cities' suburbs'.

Although 'Rembetika' is the name of the typical Greek music in general, it is now considered as distinctive of Skopelos island and its popularity has given credence to the concept that it is in fact the Greek version of the American blues.

The cadence of this beautiful music sounding in the taverns at night usually communicates 'vibes' that makes a very special atmosphere. The Skopelitis Giorgios Xintaris is one of the biggest exponents of Rembetika, and he can usually be seen performing at typical taverns and Rembetika clubs with his son, or other musician friends. When summer opens, this 'rebeti' artist usually plays in the open air restaurant placed on the top of Skopelos kastro, which he owns. Although he is one of the last remaining icons of Rembetika, other famous main stream singers, such as Eleni Tsaligopoulou and Eleutheria Arvanitaki, came out from Skopelos Rembetika clubs, which aids interest in this tradition. Kostas Kalafatis, another well known singer living on Skopelos, also performs live in various restaurants and at public events throughout the summer. He is often to be seen performing in Anna's Restaurant at the weekend. Molos restaurant has live music in the summer on Tuesday, Thursday and Saturday.

Tavernas, estiatoria and ouzeries that do not offer live performances play Giorgios Xintaris records, along with other Rembetika music, in the late evening. Cafes tend to play mainstream Greek pop and bars are eclectic in their musical tastes, but feature jazz strongly.

The night clubs of Skopelos and Glossa, which party through the night until five or six in the morning, provide a great experience, but remember that the music on offer is Greek, not mainstream European. Alcohol can also be expensive. Greeks tend to keep costs down by buying a bottle of whisky and sharing it, together with lots of water.

However, Greek music is appreciated by locals and foreigners alike, as it keeps tradition alive and contributes to the enjoyment of both locals and visitors. Skopelos also has great jazz bars, although the music tends not to be live.

Cinema

In high season, films are shown at Orfeas - the open air cinema in Skopelos Town. Seating is on directors' chairs and you can take your own refreshments, as long as you are not obvious with your alcohol. Drinks can sometimes be bought from trestle tables at the back, or from a machine. Keep your ticket in case you want to stretch your legs or run out for a pie in the interval!

Do not expect block-busters. Greek films, cultural films and children's films are shown, mostly with Greek or English sub-titles.

The cinema opens after dark and is situated on the road to the post office. Look for the metal wrought iron gate next to the shop Euromania.

A Brief History of Skopelos

Prehistory - 30,000 BC

The early history of Ancient Greece is not very detailed or clear and this period is referred to as the Dark Ages. The first people to inhabit Ancient Greece built settlements along the shoreline. They relied on the Aegean Sea for supplies and trade.

Remnants of settlements belonging to these peoples have been discovered on Alonnisos, at Kokkinokastro and Ag. Demetrius; and on Skopelos, but these have not been developed into touring sites for the general public. The graves at Sendoukia are thought to be Neolithic, as they are very similar to grave sites from this period on Evia.

Minoan and Mycenean Greece

About 2500 BC, Crete became the centre of the Aegean civilization. The Cretan Minoans dominated the region and colonized Skopelos. They founded three cities, Stafilos, Peparithos and Glossa, which is probably named after Knossos in Crete. They brought vines, olives and grain to the islands.

A volcanic eruption in 144 BC on Thera (Santorini), crushed the Minoan civilisation and their culture was absorbed by the Acheans, who built their capital at Mycenae.

According to Homer, in his epic poem 'The Iliad', around 1200 BC a conflict arose between Mycenae and Troy, involving such romantic and legendary figures as Helen, Paris and Achilles. Armed invaders hid themselves inside a large wooden horse that was proffered as a gift to the city. As the horse was brought into the city, they appeared from within the horse, attacked and seized control. Homer names Prince Stafilos, one of the sons of the god Dionysos and the Princess Ariadne of Crete, as having fought in this battle. In 1936 a rectangular shaped grave was discovered in Stafilos, on Skopelos, which brought to life the mythical Prince Stafilos. The grave contained three bodies and many treasures, the most valuable being a golden sword, which is now in the National Museum in Athens.

Ancient Greece 1000 BC - 479 BC

In ancient times, 1000BC - 479BC, the Myceanean tribes of mainland Greece drove the Cretans away from Skopelos and the island was conquered by Pelias, King of Iolkos. The temporary decline of Skopelos after this period resulted from continuous plundering by pirates.

From 800-750 BC, Skopelos was occupied by the Chalcidians. The three settlements which were then founded continued to exist until the Byzantine era: Peparithos (now Skopelos town), Panormos and Selinous (now Loutraki). Loutraki has a small information pavilion, signposted from the car park, which shows the finds from this period, now in various museums.

From the beginning of the 6th century BC, exports of wine and olive oil brought prosperity to the island, so much so that the Peparithians sent sacrificial offerings to the Delphic Oracle and minted their own silver coins.

Agnona was an ancient victor of the Olympic Games, and won the running competition in 569 BC. According to legend the victor disembarked here on his return from the games. His countrymen named the spot after him as a mark of respect and to honour him today's bay of Agnontas was given his name.

Classical Greece 479 BC-330 BC

The Persian Wars began in 490 BC, with a Persian invasion in Greece led by Darius the Great. The Greek forces crushed the invasion at Marathon, under General Miltiades. In 480 BC, the Persians launched a second attack led by Xerxes and sacked and ruined Athens. The Greeks later won a decisive military victory at Salamis, where they defeated the Persian naval fleet.

Skopelos participated in all the wars, and in 479 BC became a colony of the Athenians, establishing a democracy similar to that of Athens. It became a wine producing area, exporting throughout Greece. Aristotelis refers to the famous wine of Peparethos as being renowned for its aphrodisiac qualities. Millions of pieces of amphorae have been uncovered by archaeologists, showing the scope of Skopelos' influence.

The island became rich and minted its own silver coins. You can buy modern reproductions of them in the jewellery shops in town.

The island had three important towns, Peparithos (Skopelos Town), Panormos and Selinos (Loutraki). To honour the oracle of Delphi, the inhabitants of Peparithos dedicated a statue of the God Apollon, to celebrate beating the Kares in battle. A statue of Aphrodite was found in ancient Selinos and was donated to the Greek authorities by Constantinos Dentis.

The acropolis was built above the old port of Skopelos, with a temple of Athena where the Kastro ruins are today. Above the town, you may see a sign on the rocks which says 'coport wall'. This is the base of a large temple of Hephaistion, which was built on this site.

In 359 BC, Philip II became the King of Macedonia and eventually took control of the entire Greek peninsula. During this period, Skopelos established a healing centre to the God Asklepios, the remains of which are currently being excavated, and which was visited by supplicants from all over Greece (see Asklepion in a later section).

In 351 BC a pirate from Skopelos called Sostratos captured Alonnisos from the Athenians. Philip of Macedon reclaimed the island. In 341 BC, Skopelos again invaded Alonnisos and Phillip's Navy was sent to remove them a second time. An uneasy truce began between the island and Macedonia, until the battle of Chaironia in 338 BC, when the island of Skopelos passed completely to the control of the Macedonians.

The Alexandrian Empire and the Hellenistic Age

Philip II unified most of the city-states of mainland Greece under Macedonian hegemony. Then, in 336 BC, he was assassinated and Skopelos became part of the empire of Alexander III of Macedon, also known as Alexander the Great (356 BC – 323 BC).

Usually taken to begin with the death of Alexander, the Hellenistic period was characterized by a new wave of Greek colonization ushering in centuries of Greek settlement and cultural influence over distant areas.

Roman Greece

Roman entanglement in the Balkans began with trade. Piratical raids on Roman merchants twice led to a Roman task force invading Illyria. Tension between Macedon and Rome increased when the young king of Macedon, Philip V, harboured one of the chief pirates, Demetrius of Pharos.

On Skopelos, the present Loutraki is built over the old ruins of Selenious, which was destroyed by the Macedonians at this time because they did not want the town to fall into the hands of the Romans. The war ended with a decisive Roman victory at the Battle of Cynoscephalae (197 BC). The result was the end of Macedon as a major power in the Mediterranean.

The town of Selinous was rebuilt with no expense spared and became renowned as a tourist resort for the elite. During the Roman period, the town was at its most prosperous. Many tombs of rich merchants have been found in the area, built with materials brought from the area of Assos, located in what is now Turkey. This in itself shows the wealth of Selinous during this period.

The ruins of the marketplace of Selinous are still to be seen, as well as marble columns in front of the old Hotel Avra. To the East are the ruins of the ancient Roman baths beside Katakalou beach. In 1865, a local man discovered a statue of Athena which is now in the National Archaeological Museum in Athens. Many other artefacts have been discovered and they are now in the Archaeological Museum in Volos.

Byzantine and Crusader Greece

The division of the Roman Empire in 330 AD brought Skopelos under Byzantine rule: As part of the Eastern Empire of Rome, Greece was ruled from Constantinople. When the Eastern Roman Empire was succeeded by the Byzantine Empire in the 4th century, Greece, and Skopelos along with it, became Orthodox in religion. In 347 AD, Righinos is mentioned as the Bishop of Skopelos and subsequently its patron saint.

Byzantine evidence can be seen all over the island, in the legacy of hundreds of churches and a wealth of religious art.

The ancient name of Peparithos began slowly to give way to the new name, Skopelos, which means rocky. The name Skopelos appeared for the first time in texts that Ptolemy wrote in the 2nd century AD and is probably due to the many reefs around the island. However, the two names co-existed until the 11th century. Skopelos and Loutraki, because of their status as ports, were the most important towns at this time.

The island of Skopelos was allowed to be self governed and served as a place of exile until 1204, when the Byzantine Empire was divided among the leaders of the Fourth Crusade after they conquered Constantinople. Skopelos was ruled by the Ghisi, a family of Venetian merchants, who were also in charge of Mykonos and Tinos.

Venice had no large army, but had a powerful fleet, so the strategy to retain the Greek possessions was based on building fortresses which could resist Turkish attack until help could arrive from the sea. The Kastro was built at this time, on the site of the ancient acropolis. The Ghisi tower ensured control over the bay and it was protected by a maze of very narrow and steep streets, often interrupted by low arches. The whole town became a fortified stronghold with the Kastro at its centre. In the old Venetian quarter - the Frangomachalas - are still preserved some of the old, imposing castle-houses.

Constantinople and Mystras were recovered by the Byzantine Greeks in 1261 and, in 1276, Skopelos returned under the often nominal rule of the reconstituted Byzantine Empire. Piracy became dominant. In 1457 the Turks seized Constantinople and the inhabitants of Skopelos asked for Venetian protection. In 1538 Khayr al Din (Barbarossa - *red beard*), corsair and admiral of the Turkish fleet, seized Skopelos. The town was destroyed and the people enslaved. The Folk Museum houses an impressive collection of weapons, tools and equipment from pirate ships that ravaged the area at this time.

Venetian and Ottoman Greece

The Ottoman Turks conquered almost all remaining Greek territory by 1460. For the next 350 years, the Greek state officially ceased to exist. Rebellious bands of brigands and private militias were formed, especially on the islands.

In 1600 those who had managed to escape from the attack of Barbarossa, into Euboia and Thessaly, began to arrive on Skopelos once more. Ottoman rule began, but Turkish influence was weak. The inhabitants elected their own elders and had their own laws. They were only obliged to send to the Kapoudhan Pasha, the Admiral of Constantinople, thirty sailors to serve for one year in the Naval Station. There has never been a Turkish settlement on the island, although Turkish influence can be seen in terms of local architecture and decoration. The island began to prosper again. Greek merchants traded throughout the Ottoman Empire and Skopelos became rich as a ship building island.

The island became so important that it had consulates representing the

Great Powers. The Consul of Great Britain was Stephanos Dhapontes, who also represented Great Britain in Skiathos and Alonnisos. Dhapontes was born on Skopelos in 1714 and received his early education on the island. He became a monk, taking the name Kaesarios and lived for three years on the islet of Piperi (Pepper) close to Skopelos and in the Evangelistrias Monastery on Skopelos.

He founded a school, which he named Akademia (after Plato's Academy in Athens), situated by the church with the clock tower. For about a decade, while the educated monk Lerotheos from Athos taught there, the school flourished. Rich families from all over Europe sent their children here to be educated. After that, it declined and eventually ceased to exist.

Dapontes went to Athos in 1765 and lived in the Xiropotamou and Koutloumousiou Monasteries up to 1778. He then came to live in the Evangelistrias Abbey (which he himself had founded) on Skopelos where he stayed until 1784, before returning to Athos to die. During his lifetime, he wrote many thousands of articles, poems and treatises, which are still published today.

The War of Independence

In the mid 18th century, groups of Greek revolutionaries from mainland Greece began to arrive on Skopelos. When, in 1770, the Russian Admiral Alexander Orloff sailed the Aegean to incite the Greeks to an uprising, Skopeliti sailors served with him. As a mark of respect to the Skopeliti sailor who led him to the Port of Tsesme, where the whole Turkish fleet was destroyed, Orloff presented a bell to Skopelos, which is now in the church of tou Christou.

In 1803, Skopelos had 35 ships with a volume of 6300 tons, 525 sailors and 140 ships' cannons. From 1805 on, Skopelites fought in the ranks of the armed Greek revolutionaries, from bases on Skopelos and Skiathos. They attacked Turkish bases in the Aegean, in Chalkidiki and Magnesia.

The Greek flag was raised on March 25th, 1821, marking the beginning of the struggle for independence. Throughout 1821-1826, the ships of Skopelos assisted revolutionaries wherever they were needed.

After the suppression of the Revolution of Chalkidiki, Olympos and Thessaly, 70,000 refugees escaped to Skopelos. The situation became critical and fights broke out over provisions and food.

In 1828 Kapodistrias was elected governor of the Greek State and took immediate action to stamp out piracy, which thrived in the Sporades. The islands then came under the administration of the Greek State in the Protocol of London on February 3rd 1830.

Pavlos Nirvanas (the pseudonym of the author Petros K. Apostolidi) was born in 1866 in Russia. His first poetic collection was published in 1884 and he then published a column in newspapers. From then onwards he produced poems, short stories, fiction novels, essays, columns and cinematographic scripts. He died in Athens in 1937.

Nirvanas' father was from Skopelos and his mother from Chios. His house in Skopelos town has been restored and is being created as a new museum. Pablo's bar on the Paralea above the restaurant 'Ta Kimata' is named in his honour.

In 1878, the Greek State used Skopelos as a base to fight for the independence of Thessaly, which was still under Ottoman rule. During this period, the Turks called the Sporades 'the islands of the Devil'. In 1898, the Turks were gone, never to return.

The Greek War of Independence marked the overthrow of the Ottomans and the start of the 'Great Idea'. This was to bring all Greek people under one flag. During the 19th century the Greeks succeeded in doubling their national territory and reasserting sovereignty over many of the islands. However, an attempt to recover Constantinople after World War I, ended in disaster for Greece. In 1922 millions of Greeks were expelled from Smyrna in Turkish Anatolia, ending thousands of years of Greek occupation in Asia Minor.

Modern Greece

With the invention of steam ships, the master boat builders of Skopelos lost their supremacy and the island's economy was badly damaged.

The years after the 1922 defeat by Turkey were terrible ones for the Greek people. The influx of refugees contributed to the political instability of the inter-war years and tens of thousands of refugees arrived in Skopelos at this period, many of them starving.

The new centralised Greek State neglected Skopelos and the island was left to its own devices, except that during the first decade of the twentieth century, Skopelos was used once again as a place of exile for political dissenters.

Phyloxera struck and destroyed the vineyards of the island in the 1940's. Poorer islanders were obliged to pledge their land as security for loans. In many cases, the land was forfeited, a method by which some of the very large estates on the island today were amassed.

In Athens, the dictatorship of Metaxas was followed by invasion in 1940. During the Second World War, the island was first occupied by the Italians (June 1941 - September 1943) and then the Germans (September 1943 - October 1944). British soldiers were sheltered in the caves by the monastery of Taxiarchon. Vangelis Hannas, a former mayor of Skopelos who died in 2010, remembered smuggling them from the mainland and hiding them there until the islanders could get them on a ship to neutral Turkey. Vangelis was arrested by the occupying Italian forces but was released after the local people marched on their headquarters.

The last German troops evacuated mainland Greece in 1944 and the church bells of the island rang joyfully to inform the people. However, Greece immediately fell into a brutal four year civil war. The island did not escape some of the trauma of these events and members of the community who fought against the Italians and Germans were forced to leave. Only recently have their names been added to the cenotaph on the Paralea. The population of Skopelos was further depleted by migration to America, Australia and Athens.

After experiencing the Cyprus problem in the 1950s and the military dictatorship of 1967 to 1974, Greece is now an established democracy and a member of the European Union. Having stagnated until the 1980's, when it was designated a world heritage site, Skopelos is again becoming prosperous. Young people now remain here, or return after they have completed their studies. Tourism is the main industry, but traditional methods of agriculture and fishing mean the island is once again becoming a place proud of its heritage.

Museums

Folklore Museum - Skopelos

The building that houses the Skopelos Folklore Museum today was donated by the Nikolaidis family in 1991. The original old mansion was built in 1795 and the house, with its exhibition rooms, give a great example of life as it might have been in Skopelos over 200 years ago. Visitors to the museum can travel back in time and gain insight into the lifestyle of the mansion's owners.

With a recent interior facelift of the rooms, the museum exhibits a rich collection of handmade embroideries, traditional costumes and ceramics, all in the finest condition. The rooms are decorated just as they could have been when the family lived there, and are furnished with original hand-carved wooden furniture along with paintings and photographs by local artists. On exhibition is the bridal bed-chamber including the Skopelos Wedding dress. The folklore museum has an excellent collection of pottery, knives, models of small ships, paintings and other fascinating objects made by the islanders. A small charge is made for admission.

The Vakrata Museum – Skopelos

This museum is set in an old and substantial family house, donated to the municipality of Skopelos in 1995 by the Vakrata family. The members of the family were of the professional classes and the daughters were the first women to study at the university of Athens at the beginning of the 19th century. Cultured and well-travelled, the family created a home bursting with artifacts gathered from around the world. The museum today houses only those things preserved by the family and is positively bulging with treasures, presenting a comprehensive picture of a nineteenth century home in Greece. There is also a large and very important private collection of family icons, coveted by the icon museum of Athens, but retained here on Skopelos according to the wishes of the family.

The house and all its contents have been restored purely by volunteers, in a programme begun in October 2008. There is a small entrance fee. The museum is situated up the steep hill beside the Ambrosia sweet shop on the Paralea.

Museum of Cultural Heritage - Glossa

The Museum of Cultural Heritage and the Library 'Perseus Athineos' opened its doors to the public in July 2008. Located in a stone house built in 1926, and renovated by local artisans, the building has a wonderful balcony from which one can see the whole village and the sea surrounding the island.

The aim of the museum is to preserve and promote the history of the island of Skopelos through naval history, documents and personal items. The museum was created with the continuous effort of individual people to make something special for their island. Completed in June 2008 and opened to the public a month later, it works under the aegis of the Hellenic Foundation and the entrance is free. Museums are closed on Sunday.

The Photographic Centre

In recent years, Skopelos, as a member of the cultural network of Greek towns, was declared the 'Town of Photography' and the Greek Photographic Centre was created here. It holds prestigious exhibitions throughout the summer, and has hosted workshops and significant retrospectives of the work of photographers Robert Capa, Herbert List and Josef Koudelka, among others.

This non-profit organisation was founded in 1995, focusing in particular on Eastern European photography. In 1996 a photography festival was held, and 178 images by the noted Czech photographer Josef Koudelka, famous for his photography of the Soviet invasion of Prague, were shown.

The museum/exhibition is held in the school hall on the road past the medical centre.

The Arts Foundation of Skopelos.

Artists particularly enjoy, and are inspired by, the beauty of the island. Many come especially to develop their skills during seminars run by organisations such as the Arts Foundation. Their work can be seen - and bought - in the several galleries in the back streets of Skopelos Town. The Arts Foundation is situated on the road up from the Kastro to Raches.

The Cultural Organisation of Skopelos

This organization has also set up music, painting, theatre and photography groups, which organise events in a busy high season calendar.

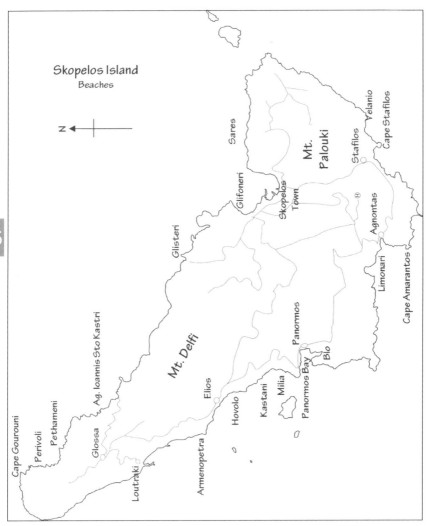

Map of the beaches on Skopelos

Beaches

Skopelos has many beaches. Many of them can be reached via the local bus service during the season, but if you have your own transport then it is possible to get off the beaten track and discover a small cove which you can enjoy all by yourself.

Do not expect sandy beaches, although there are some on the island. Most beaches are shingle and few are commercialised - you will not get 'kiss me quick' hats, candy floss and amusements at all, and on some of the main beaches, expect only sunbeds, sunshades and a kiosk to buy drinks if you are lucky. However, it is possible to stroll along some beaches and have a meal in a good taverna, or a cooling drink by the sea.

Most of the beaches on Skopelos are situated in the south west of the island and are either pebbly or a mixture of fine shingle and sand. The north east coast is rugged and inhospitable and its coves are easier to approach by boat.

Beaches around Skopelos

Skopelos Town

The town's long, sand and shingle beach looks very inviting in high season, since that part of the Paralea has been developed. Facing north against the prevailing summer wind, it attracts more than its fair share of flotsam, but it is cleaned by the owners of the bars which have opened on the beach. Restaurants now have tables along the walkway and the whole area feels more cosmopolitan (high season only).

Fresh water from a covered culvert trickles into the sea and in the spring, many wading birds can be observed pecking their way along the beach.

Glifoneri

Glifoneri is within walking distance of the town: Follow the road uphill from the Kastro area for about 20 metres and then take a right fork down to a small shingle beach lined by a few tavernas.

Glisteri

This is a secluded shingle beach north of the port, in a sheltered bay approached by a long track, about 3 km from Skopelos town. In high season taxi boats run from Skopelos town to Glisteri beach about 2 or 3 times a day.

There is a small stone and shingle beach set in a deep and secluded bay with especially fresh fish, and they make the place a pleasant spot for that seashore meal. The arch from Donna's House in the film has been moved from its former site and rebuilt here for fans of 'Mamma Mia!'

Agnontas

There is a very narrow strip of sand and shingle in front of the tavernas. The beach shelves gently into the sea, protected by the steep hills on either side of the bay so it is safe for children, although sea urchins are a nuisance. The beach turns to stone and shingle as you head around the bay and there is plenty of shade from trees that come right down to the shoreline. There are no sun beds.

There is a mini market and a small tourist kiosk opens in the summer. Several small hotels and apartments have appeared in recent years and there is a regular bus service available, as well as taxis.

Just south of Agnontas on the road to Stafilos is a dirt track which branches though the forest leading to several secluded small coves at Amarantos, the 'Little Island' of 'Mamma Mia!' - actually a small promontory on the coast. Pines sweep right down to the water's edge offering privacy, shade and - so visitors claim - freedom from the wasps that can plague the island.

Limonari

This large crescent of white sand is considered one of the best beaches on the island. You can also reach it by road - about 9km from Skopelos Town - although the bus stops some half-mile away at Alikias making for a dusty walk along a dirt track. The long, wide beach is of sharp white sand and it can shelve steeply into the water in places. There is a sloping slab of slippery rock the length of the beach that keeps the water crystal clear but forces bathers to slide in and out of the water on their behinds. Not elegant but it works!

The sand is so white it can be almost blinding at midday and the underwater reflections can turn the sea a dazzling turquoise. Two waterside tavernas offer the basics and one has installed a swimming pool.

Panormos

Panormos is a large sheltered bay which becomes very busy in high season. There are a number of tavernas and it is possible to rent a boat from here. As the name suggests, Panormos is a beach with a view. The road threads through pine trees to a magnificent wide, sheltered bay riddled with small and secluded inlets reached by paths over the rocks, or by wading or swimming through the water along the shoreline.

The beach is ideal for swimming; no sand anywhere but plenty of pebbles and they shelve pretty sharply into the sea. The sea also tends to be colder in this area than other Skopelos beaches.

Access is directly off the main road and there is plenty of parking space. Buses and taxis also call in from Skopelos Town - about 12km away.

There are several lively tavernas along the shore offering ranks of sun beds. There are also a few shops and a couple of mini markets to serve the growing numbers of hotels and apartments that have sprung up in the area.

Panormos was once the site of an ancient city and sections of old wall can still be seen.

Walking through the woods west of Panormos and towards Milia will take you to the area known as **ADRINA,** where there are many small and isolated coves of shingle, often deserted and enclosed by pines.

Land beside the hotel has been sold off and is now fenced, preventing access from the road. The only access now is a footpath from the northern end of Panormos beach or by boat.

Milia

Milia is one of the finest beaches on the island; three silver swathes of treelined pebble and sand, crystal clear waters and a large taverna by the central beach. There is a beach bar and sun beds.

The beach lies north of Panormos, over the headland, about 14km southwest of Skopelos Town and a similar distance east from Glossa, the island's second largest village. Access is down a dirt track off the main road, where there is a car park. There are buses and taxis from both Skopelos Town and Glossa, but you have to walk about 500m from the main road to the beach if you take the bus.

If the main beaches gets too crowded there is a small cove to the north that is not often visited and, out to sea is the small, pine clad island of Dasia which is easily reached by boat.

Kastani

Another kilometre walk to the north brings you to Kastani, a pleasant sand and fine shingle beach. You can get a car down to it but you may have trouble turning around. A beach cantina sometimes springs up in the summer but there are no other facilities.

A small jetty appeared briefly but it was only a mock-up, built for the movie set of Mamma Mia. It has since, like the film crews and movie stars, vanished, leaving no trace.

Further along the coast north of Milia are several more coves, all quite difficult to get to, being away from the main road and usually visited by those who have hired a boat. All are stone and shingle and their main attraction lies is in their peace and seclusion.

The best are just north of Kastani at **NERAKI** and **FTELIA**, each side of a small and attractive bay, and further north **EKATOPENINDARI** and eventually **HOVOLO** which is on the outskirts of Elios.

Beaches around Glossa

At **Spilia** there is a cave and the small monastery of **Agios Ioannis** perched high on rocks overlooking a spectacular headland above a double coved beach. The headland was created when the cliffs collapsed into the sea and the chapel of the monastery featured strongly in the hit movie musical 'Mamma Mia!'

The monastery of the **Agion Taxiarchon** is built on the remains of a 7th century Byzantine church and the **Gourouni Cape** has a lighthouse.

Other roads and tracks lead down to deserted beaches. On the northwest coast are **MYRTIA** and **KOUTRIA**, while to the east are pebble coves at **PERIVOLI, PETHAMENI, HONDROGIORGI, KERAMOTO, MAVRAKI** and **SPILIA**. Like all remote north coast beaches they are prone to collect sea wrack. Many are difficult to find and only Spilia and Perivoli have roads leading to them.

Pethameni is at the bottom of a steep and precipitous path but has a small beach and some good snorkelling. **Hondrogiorgi** has easier access and so is popular with locals at weekends.

There are many other coves and small beaches not described in the limited space here.

Kastani beach - the setting for Donna's beach bar in 'Mamma Mia!'

A Little Bit of Greek

The Greek language is considered to be one of the most difficult languages to learn. However, Greek words are used all the time in the English language and a great percentage of medical terminology is also Greek. So you are almost fluent in Greek already!

These pages are not going to teach you how to speak Greek but you can learn some basic Greek words and phrases in order to impress your friends on Skopelos.

As happens in nearly every country, people on Skopelos will be glad to hear you trying to speak their language. Even if all you can say is 'kalimera' or 'Yassou', people will smile and open up. A little bit of Greek goes a long way! Local people really appreciate your efforts even if you just greet them in their language. So we have listed below a few words for you to try out - you will find using them, however wrongly, a great icebreaker. They are written out phonetically for easier pronunciation. Remember, in Greek **all** letters are pronounced.

Learn Greetings in Greek :

In all the following, 'e' is read as in 'egg' and 'th' is read as in "this". The emphasis in pronunciation falls on the syllable which is in underlined script

Kalim**e**ra - good morning - καλημέρα. Used both when coming to and going away from a place.

Kalisp**e**ra - good afternoon - καλησπέρα. Used only when coming to a place or meeting someone in the evening or at night.

Kalin**i**hta - good night - καληνύχτα. Used only as a goodbye greeting in the evening or at night.

h**e**rete (e as in egg) - hello - χαίρετε, used between 10:00 and 14:00

y**a**ssou - hello or goodbye - γειά σου (greeting to one person or a friend)

y**a**ssas - hello or goodbye - γειά σας (greeting to more persons or a more formal and polite way to greet an unknown person)

ad**i**o - goodbye - αντίο

Y**a**ssou f**i**le mou N**i**ko - Hello my friend Niko -- an easy way to please a Greek friend of yours.

Learn the names of Towns and Places in Greece

In all the following, 'e' is read as in 'egg' and 'th' is read as in 'this'. The emphasis in pronunciation falls on the syllable which is in underlined script .

Ell**a**tha	Greece	Ελλάδα
Ellin**as**	Greek (man)	Έλληνας
Ellin**it**ha	Greek (woman)	Ελληνίδα
Ath**in**a	Athens	Αθήνα

Learn the Greek Numbers:

0	zero	mith**en**	μηδέν
1	one	**e**na	ένα (m: ένας, f: μία, n: ένα)
2	two	th**i**o	δύο
3	three	tr**i**a	τρία (m: τρεις, f: τρεις, n: τρία)
4	four	t**e**ssara	τέσσερα
			(m:τέσσερις, f:τέσσερις, n:τέσσερα)
5	five	p**e**nte	πέντε
6	six	**e**xi	έξι
7	seven	ept**a**	επτά or εφτά
8	eight	okt**o**	κτώ or οχτώ
9	nine	enn**i**a	εννέα or εννιά
10	ten	d**e**ka	δέκα
11	eleven	**e**ndeka	έντεκα
12	twelve	d**o**deka	δώδεκα
13	thirteen	dekatr**i**a	δεκατρία
14	fourteen	dekat**e**ssera	δεκατέσσερα
15	fifteen	dekap**e**nte	δεκαπέντε
16	sixteen	deka**e**xi	δεκαέξι or δεκάξι
17	seventeen	dekaept**a**	δεκαεπτά or δεκαεφτά
18	eighteen	dekaokt**o**	δεκαοκτώ or δεκαοχτώ
19	nineteen	dekaenn**e**a	δεκαεννέα or δεκαεννιά
20	twenty	**ee**kosi	είκοσι

Learn the colours in Greek

Aspro	white	άσπρο
Lefko	white	λευκό
Mavro	black	μαυρό
Gri	grey	γκρι
Kokkino	red	κόκκινο
Kitrino	yellow	κίτρινο
Prassino	green	πράσινο
Kafe	brown	καφέ
Mov	purple	μωβ
Galazio	light blue	γαλάζιο
Ble	blue	μπλε

Learn Common Greek Phrases

In all the following, 'e' is read as in 'egg' and 'th' is read as in 'this'. The emphasis in pronunciation falls on the syllable which is in underlined script.

Efharisto	Thank you
Parakalo	You're Welcome
Milate Anglika?	Do you speak English?
Then katalaveno	I don't understand
Pos se lene?	What is your name?
Me lene …	My name is …
Apo pou eisai?	Where are you from?
Eimai apo Anglia	I am from England
Thelo ena kafe	I want a coffee
Thelo ena tsai	I want a tea
Thelo mia bira	I want a beer
Thelo ena poto	I want a drink
Thelo ena thomatio	I want a room
Ehete thomatio?	Do you have a room?
ya mia mera	for one day
ya thio meres	for two days
ya mia evthomatha	for one week
ya thio evthomathes	for two weeks
Poso kanei?	How much is it?
Poso hrostao	How much do I owe?
Logariasmo parakalo	The bill, please.
Boro na bgalo mia fotografia?	May I take a photo?

Ela	Come
Fiye	Go away!
	(fi as in fish, ye as in yellow)
Ise **o**morfi	You are beautiful
M' **a**reseis	I like you
S' agap**o**	I love you
M' agap**as**?	Do you love me?
Ag**a**pi mou	My love, Darling
Fil**i**se me	Kiss me
F**i**li	Kiss
F**i**los/Fil**i**	Friend (male)/(female). Pay attention to the small difference from 'kiss'
Eho f**i**lo	I have a boyfriend
Eimai pantrem**ee**ni	I am married (female)

The Greek Alphabet and the sounds of the Greek letters

A	α	a	N	ν	n	
B	β	v as in vital	Ξ	ξ	x or ks	
Γ	γ	similar to y in yard	O	o	o	
Δ	δ	th as in this	Π	π	p	
E	ε	e as in egg	P	ρ	r	
Z	ζ	z as in zebra	Σ	σ	s	
H	η	e as in era	T	τ	t	
Θ	θ	th as in throne	Y	υ	e as in era	
I	ι	e as in era	Φ	φ	f	
K	κ	k	X	χ	h as in he	
Λ	λ	l	Ψ	ψ	ps	
M	μ	m	Ω	ω	o	

Finally, sign language is an essential part of the Greek way of communicating, so a quick scribble mime will speedily get you your bill!

Festivals and Celebrations

Approximately 97% of the Greek population are Greek Orthodox, belonging to a sacramental Church which is under the control of its clergy, who also have an enormous say in governmental affairs.

The Greek Year

Most of the Greek customs and traditions still present in the 21st century stem from the Greek Orthodox religion. The Orthodox Church calendar begins on September 1st and ends on August 31st. Each day is sacred: each is a saint's day, as at least one saint is venerated daily.

The following is an accumulation of some of the most significant and important festivals and celebrations that are still followed avidly in Skopelos today. The actual rituals and procedures can vary from region to region and even from village to village, but this will give you an insight into the more common traditions.

Pomegranates and the first day of the year.

On the 1st of September the grape harvest begins and that is considered to be the beginning of the new year in the Orthodox calendar. So, early in the morning, the housewives fill their pots with water from a spring and head back home, or nowadays take a bottle of water and go outside the house.

Upon entering the house they will drop down a pomegranate and step on it. This brings good luck for the New Year. Then they say loudly 'Good morning house' and step inside with the right foot first. Water is then spilled in the four corners of the house and the lady of the house says 'As the water spills and rolls so will the good times roll in this house'.

Pomegranates have a long and venerable tradition in countries around the world. According to Greek mythology pomegranates symbolize death and fertility, while ancient Chinese people believed that its juice contained a 'concentrated soul' and could give immortality. Some researchers believe that Eve gave Adam a pomegranate instead of an apple. Mohamed said that the consuming of pomegranates relieves mankind from hate and envy. Homer mentions the pomegranate tree as one of the most cultivated trees of his time and says that the king of the Faiakes, Alkinoos used to cultivate many pomegranate trees. The Babylonians believed that the eating of pomegranates before a battle would make them immortal and ancient Egyptians used to bury their dead together with pomegranates.

Modern science confirms that pomegranates act against heart and encephalic diseases and high blood pressure, are a natural anti-aging medicine and increase fertility, as well as cleansing and protecting the skin.

Christmas

In Greece, for the devout, Christmas is preceded by a 40 day fast beginning on November 15th and lasting until Christmas Eve, until the first star appears. When the star is seen, people lay the table ready for the Christmas supper. On Skopelos, early in the same morning, children knock on doors of houses and shops in the neighbourhood, jangling triangles and singing songs - kalanta. They are given sweets and money.

On Christmas Day people go to church and then have a feast where everyone joins in to eat, drink and enjoy themselves. More and more often, reflecting the commercialisation of Western tradition propagated through American television, small presents are given today.

The Christmas dining table is decorated with traditional cakes and sweets and the 'christopsomo' - special bread. On Christmas Day, the male head of the household traditionally crosses the bread with a knife, offering each person at the table a piece and wishing them 'Xronia polla!'

From Christmas to Epiphany, goblins emerge from the ground to make mischief, until they are banished by the priest casting a cross on the waters of the sea on January 6th.

New Year

On New Year's Eve, the children of Skopelos go from house to house singing Carols and banging on metal triangles. In the past, the children would carry a toy boat with them, but now we only see boats in some shop windows or as part of the street light decorations. In Ancient Greece, boats on wheels were the traditional way of transporting Dionysus, the god of wine and feasting.

At the moment of the change in the year, all the lights are switched off, all the taps turned on and all the windows opened to let in the fresh air. Some women drink a glass of water as the clock strikes twelve, having previously placed it next to jewellery or money. On New Year's Day the first person across the threshold should be the master of the house, the eldest son, or another lucky child, if there is to be a good, prosperous new year. They enter the house with the right foot first, carrying a small icon of a saint, or smashing a pomegranate inside the door, whilst wishing everyone a 'Happy New Year'.

Generally, people celebrate New Year's Day having parties, visiting relatives and gambling. While they are out, they leave a tray with sweets and water for Ag. Vassilios, who is believed to visit the house and leave presents. Ag. Vassilios is the Greek name for Saint Basil, the Santa Claus of the Greeks.

Godparents give presents to Godchildren. It is unlucky on this day to break glass objects and mirrors, to quarrel, to cry, or to lose things, lest such mishaps will happen all year long.

The most important custom is cutting the 'vassilopitta'. This is a big, round cake, like a brioche, which is dedicated to Aghios Vassilios. The cake can be decorated with icing sugar, representing wishes and has a coin buried into it on the underside by the woman of the house. The family gathers round the table and the father of the house carries out the following ritual: With a knife, he makes a cross three times on the cake, wishing everyone a 'Happy New Year', before cutting it into pieces. He starts by naming each piece according to the recipient: the first piece for Jesus Christ; the second for St Basil; the next to the house; the next to the poor; then to each member of the family in turn - first the grandparents, then the parents - himself and his wife - then the children. Other relatives are served next and then friends. Whoever discovers the coin will be lucky throughout the year!

The Blessing of the Sea
Kalikantzara are little devils from the underworld, which are small and black, with pointed ears, horns, curly tails, goats' legs and human hands. They arrive on Christmas Eve and come down the chimney of everybody's house to create havoc. Their intention is to take over the world.

On the 5th of January, the first sanctification of the Epiphany (The Enlightenment) takes place in church on the eve of the holiday. The priests, each accompanied by two choir boys, holding a cross and a basil branch, visit every house in the parish and bless it, the surrounding land and its occupants. This exorcises the devils, who have nowhere to go but into the water: the sea, a river or even a reservoir.

On Skopelos, on the 6th of January, a long procession is formed and follows whatever road that leads to the sea. Up in front of the procession are the cherub icons, followed by the priests dressed in their best holiday splendour, then the VIPs, followed by all the people. The priests then perform the ceremony of 'blessing the sea.'

They throw a cross into the water, in memory of the priests who gave the icons to the protection of the sea during the Turkish Occupation, and by this action the devils are sent back to the underworld.

Then, those who dare - mostly the younger people of the village - jump into the usually icy water and compete in retrieving the cross. The one who brings the cross up to the surface will enjoy good luck and health for the entire year.

The fishing boats send up flares and sound their klaxons, after which the whole town then repairs for coffee in the cafes.

Epiphany celebrates the arrival of the three kings and their giving of gifts to the Holy Family. Therefore January 6th is the day for the proper exchange of presents and large Christmas gifts are given today.

Apocrea (Carnival)

Carnival is the three week period before 'Saracosti' (Lent) during which people stop eating meat or animal products. According to the etymological interpretation of the Greek and the Latin terms, *carne vale* or *apo crea* mean 'goodbye to meat'.

Before the Lenten period begins, people need to have fun. Special days are feast days when the last of the forbidden foods of Lent may be consumed, culminating in 'Smoky Thursday' when everybody barbeques meat in a final 'blow out' before Lent begins.

The festival comes down to us from the ancient worship of Dionysus in Greece and is a time of dancing, masquerade and wine, which loosens inhibitions and brings a mellow, cheerful mood that reaches its peak a few

Apocrea (carnival) traditional dress

days before people begin the long fast of Lent.

During the second week of **Apokries**, known as 'Kreatini' (Meat Week), meat may be eaten every day, even the traditional fast days of Wednesday and Friday.

The Thursday of the second week of carnival is known as '**Tsiknopempti**' (Smokey Thursday). This is when the festivities begin. Traditionally, everyone must cook meat so that the smoke or 'tsikna' fills the air and everybody knows it's a feast-day. On Tsiknopempti the first masqueraders make their appearance and the first carnival parties are held. Bars, clubs and restaurants are packed and parties are 'gate-crashed' by marauding revellers.

The third week is called '**Tyrini**' (Cheese Week). People can eat dairy products and fish but not meat. On Sunday, men in the various neighbourhoods of Skopelos dress up, blacken (or blue!) their faces and build boats from rubbish. These are dragged through the streets to the sea, where they are launched and promptly sink. The sole purpose of the exercise seems to be to get as drunk as possible whilst having a good time without the presence of women!

The Sunday before the last day of Lent, here on Skopelos the islanders still celebrate the **Vlaki Wedding**. The groom is a woman dressed as a man and the bride is a man dressed as a woman. Everyone else wears national costume or carnival dress; often cross-dressing. A procession begins midway through the morning, with more and more people joining as it parades through the town, until everyone meets on the Paralea for dancing, drinking wine and singing ribald songs.

Apokria ends on '**Kathari Deftera**' (Clean Monday), the first day of Lent.

According to current thinking, carnival has its roots in ancient ceremonies meant to help the earth put forth shoots. The magical aid took the form of leaping dances and various kinds of folk mummery and disguise, in order to propitiate harmful spirits. Down the centuries some of the ancient ceremonies and traditions have been lost, but most have been incorporated into the Christian religion and taken on a different meaning.

In ancient Greece, the festival in honour of Dionysus took place in early Spring, as Dionysus symbolised life's rebirth after Winter. Today, carnival is held in the same period but not on a fixed date, as it depends on the moveable feast of Easter.

Saracosti (Lent)

The first day of Lent begins on Ash or Clean Monday. On this day, the 'koulouma' are held. Everybody goes off to the countryside, eats Lenten food and flies kites. All their sins and unhappiness are projected onto the kite and cast to the winds, so that they may begin Lent in a cleansed state. Then the housewives wash all the grease from their kitchens, pans and utensils, before putting them away until after the Lenten fast is over.

For those who fast, Lent passes very slowly. In the past, people would cut out a figure of a woman who had no mouth (because Lady Saracosti never stops fasting) and whose hands were joined together in prayer. She had seven legs, one for each week. Every Saturday they would cut off one leg, the last one being removed on Saturday of Holy Week.

Before Easter

Easter, or as the Greeks call it 'Pascha', is the most important religious festival in the Greek Orthodox Calendar.

In the Orthodox religion, every Sunday is dedicated to the resurrection of the Lord, but 100 days are dedicated to Easter: 50 days before the festival and 50 after it to commemorate the glory of God. Easter is therefore considered the 'Feast of Feasts'.

On the Saturday before Holy Week, the Resurrection of Lazarus is celebrated. On Lazarus' Saturday, children are given traditional bread rolls, called 'lazarakia', which have the shape of a man wrapped in a shroud—the forerunner of the gingerbread man.

This day, together with Palm Sunday, holds a unique position in the church year. They are days of joy and triumph between the penitence of Great Lent and the mourning of Holy Week.

On Palm Sunday the churches are decorated with palm and bay branches. They are placed into the icon stand of the house for luck. People believe in the power of life and fertility that the palm tree passes on to women, animals and plants.

Great Week (Holy Week)

Every evening throughout Holy Week (Great Week), all the churches are decorated with purple bands. Priests dress in dark vestments and church bells keep tolling. Weddings, christenings, balls and celebrations are not to take place during this week.

On **Great Tuesday**, housewives make sweet rolls called 'koulourakia'.

On **Great Wednesday** they clean the house, then in the evening they go to church for the blessing of the Holy Oil. Everyone is encouraged to come forward for anointing with the special oil which gives spiritual as well as physical healing. People sometimes keep the blessed oil of the sick in their homes.

Great Thursday is the day for dyeing hard boiled eggs. The egg is a symbol of life and red the colour of life (as in blood). In Byzantine times, it was the custom to bake ring-breads with a red egg in the middle. These are still made and sold in supermarkets and bakeries across the island.

In the evening, after the reading of the gospel, women undertake the decoration of the bier of Christ (epitaphios) with garlands of white and purple flowers in all the most important churches of the island. Flower shops are open until after midnight and the women work through the night.

On **Great Friday** in the morning, the image of the body of Christ is taken down from the cross and placed on the bier. On Great Friday noon, all Greek flags fly at half mast.

On Great Friday evening, the service of the Epitaph, which symbolizes the funeral of Christ, is held. Then everybody follows the procession of the Epitaph, carrying brown lighted candles. The procession begins and ends at the church, following a fixed itinerary through the town. Each procession meets the congregation from the next church along the route, until all the churches process together along the Paralea, before returning the biers to the churches from which they came.

Easter Saturday/Sunday

On Holy Saturday evening, the Resurrection mass takes place, reaching its climax at midnight, with church bells pealing joyously and firework displays. All the boats in the harbour sound their horns and set off flares.

The ceremony of lighting candles from the flame of the Holy Light is the most significant moment of the year. People kiss and exchange wishes for the day, telling each other 'Christos Anesti!' which means 'Christ is risen!' To which is the reply 'Alithea Anesti!' – 'He is truly risen!'.

Then they carefully carry home their lighted candles aflame with the Holy Light of the Resurrection. Before entering their houses they make a cross with the smoke of the candle on top of the door, before lighting the oil candle before their icon stand. This light must be kept burning throughout the year.

Finally on Holy Saturday, the ceremonies come to a close as people begin to break their fasts, savouring specially prepared dishes such as 'margeirista' soup, made of lambs' innards, and cracking their red eggs. Restaurants are full all over town, as people eat through the night.

What is left of the day is then spent preparing for the big lamb feast on Easter Sunday afternoon!

May/June

The Monday of **Ayio Pnevma** (the Holy Spirit, Whit Monday in UK) marks the descent of the Holy Spirit to the assembled disciples, fifty days after Easter. Usually a modest liturgy is celebrated at rural chapels of the Holy Spirit, gaily decked out with pennants. Look out for them on Skopelos.

The Nativity of St John the Baptist

24th June celebrates one of the oldest festivals of the Christian church. It comes three months after the celebration on March 25th of the Annunciation, when the Archangel Gabriel told Mary that her cousin Elizabeth was in her sixth month of pregnancy, and six months before the Christmas celebration of the birth of Jesus. It is a day of rest and, like Christmas, is celebrated with three Masses: a vigil, at dawn, and at midday.

Metamorfosis tou Sotiros (Transfiguration of the Saviour)

August 6th is the Feast of the Transfiguration. It is celebrated throughout the island. In Skopelos Town, people take part in a traditional evening concert, dressed in national costume and singing and dancing on the Paralea.

Apokismisis tis Panagia (the Assumption of the Blessed Mary)

August 15th is the third most important religious holiday in Greece, after Easter and Christmas. This is when the tourist season here on Skopelos reaches its peak. Everyone goes to their ancestral home for the Festival and all the businesses will be closed on that day. The entire country is virtually shut down as the Greeks head for the islands and everyone takes advantage of the long weekend to rest or to light a candle for **Panagia** (the Virgin Mary) whose ascent to the heavens is commemorated during this day.

For this reason, August is the most crowded and most expensive month across the whole of Greece. The weather is very hot (with temperatures reaching $100°F/37.8°C$ on some days), the beaches crowded and the festivals in full swing.

Ferries and flights are also very crowded and the transportation system can seem to get jammed around August 15th. Don't expect to be able to book a room or a flight/ferry at the last minute: make sure to book well in advance.

Apocrea (carnival) procession through the Old Town, Skopelos

Saints' Days and Holidays

In addition to the specific dates mentioned, there are literally scores of local festivals, or paniyiria, celebrating the patron saint of the main village church. With hundreds of possible name-saints' days (calendars list two or three, often obscure, for each day) you're unlikely to travel around Skopelos for long without stumbling on something.

It is important to remember the concept of the **paramoni**, which is the eve of the festival. Most of the events listed below are celebrated on the night before, so if you show up on the morning of the date given you will very probably have missed any music, dancing or drinking.

Every orthodox Greek is named after a saint. This is obligatory if the child is going to be baptized. This means, that on each saint's day, thousands of Greeks celebrate their name days. For a list of name days celebrated each month, check out MADRO Travel website – news.

Generally, the name day is more celebrated than the birthday, and part of the celebration involves offering sweets to those around you and having some sort of party. If someone you know is having his or her name day, the appropriate thing to say to them is **'XRONIA POLLA!',** meaning 'MANY YEARS!'.

Protochronia - New Year's Day (See section on festivals and celebrations)

January 6th - Epiphany (See section on festivals and celebrations)

February 25th Agios Righinos: The patron saint of Skopelos.

Ag. Righinos was an educated Greek man with a strong desire to live a Christian life. The people of Skopelos heard of his piety and sought to make Righinos their bishop. During the rule of the Emperor Julian (361-363 AD) the Governor of Greece visited the island and requested the Bishop to renounce his faith. Righinos refused and was executed, along with at least forty other inhabitants of Skopelos, in the year 362 A.D. The spot is marked by a small shrine standing opposite the T-junction where the road from town joins the ring road.

March 25th Independence Day and the Feast of the Annunciation.
Greek National Day, March 25th, is both a national (revolution against the

Turks) and religious holiday (The Feast of the Annunciation). March 25th is the nameday for Vangelis or Evangelos and Vangelio or Evangelia or Eva. The day is celebrated with pride not just in Greece itself, but in every Greek community around the world.

Greek National Day is a big day for the children of Skopelos. It's a great opportunity for them to learn the history behind the Independence Day, as well as aspects such as dance, food, community and religion which play an important part in Greek culture. This passing on of Greek traditions to the next generation is an important responsibility for most Greek families.

In Skopelos, as in in every town and village throughout Greece, there is a school flag parade. All the schools take part and march along the Paralea, with the chosen honour student carrying the flag. There is also a big armed forces parade in Thessaloniki, in the north of Greece.

April 23rd The Feast of Ag. Georgios: Saint George's Day

Ag. Georgios, the patron saint of Greece and of shepherds, is a big rural celebration, with much feasting and dancing at associated shrines. If April 23rd falls before Easter, i.e. during Lent, the festivities are postponed until the Monday after Easter.

May Day - Protomayia

May 1st has always been celebrated in Greece as the victory of Summer over Winter, and of life over death. Traditionally, Skopelos, with its strong agricultural roots, gives the May Day festival an importance almost rivaling that of Easter Sunday itself and spit-roasted lamb is again on the menu in the countryside.

May First is also International Workers Day, a holiday first popularized by the Soviet Union. While it has lost many of its communist associations, it still is vigorously celebrated in former Soviet-bloc countries and other places in Europe. You can expect worker's groups and unions to be active today; major strikes are sometimes scheduled for May Day.

Since May Day corresponds with the peak of the flower season, flower shows and festivals are common. The ancient Minoans are believed to have celebrated one of their two 'New Year' celebrations about this time - the other was in October.

One very common commemoration is the making of a May wreath which is hung on doorways, balconies, in chapels, and many other places. Keep an eye out for them.

June 21st is the day to celebrate the summer solstice. It is the moment at which the sun is in the highest place, the longest day of the year and the shortest night.

June is the sixth month of the current Gregorian calendar and the first month of summer. It is a time when the children of Skopelos rejoice as their long summer vacation from school begins. Originally dedicated to the Goddess Hera, patron of the female sex, and sacred to all gods and goddesses who preside over love, passion, and beauty, this month is considered an excellent month for marriages.

August 6th - Metamorfosis (See section on festivals and celebrations)

August 15th - Apokismisis tis Panagia (the Assumption of the Blessed Mary) (See section on festivals and celebrations)

September 14th, the Day of the Holy Cross, is considered an important date for farming activities in Greece. The priest gives basil leaves to the faithful and farmers take a mixture of all the seeds they intend to sow, to have then blessed by the priest.

On **October 28th, Ochi Day** is commemorated. Expect to encounter parades and other celebrations commemorating Ochi Day, the anniversary of General Ioannis Metaxas' flat denial to the Italians' request for free passage to invade Greece. In October 1940 Italy, backed by Hitler, wanted to occupy Greece; Metaxas simply responded **'Ochi!'** – **'No!'** in Greek. It was a 'No!' that brought Greece into the war on the Allied side; for a time, Greece was Britain's *only* ally against Hitler.

On Skopelos, the day belongs to the school children, who gather at the cenotaph to be reminded of their history and then march down the Paralea to the applause of their families and friends.

November 17th - The Athens Polytechnic uprising in 1973 was a massive demonstration of popular rejection of the military junta, a regime which abolished civil rights, dissolved political parties and exiled, imprisoned and tortured politicians and citizens based on their political beliefs. The uprising began on November 14th, 1973, escalated to an open anti-junta revolt and ended in bloodshed in the early morning of November 17th after a series of events starting with a tank crashing through the gates of the Polytechnic.

This day is currently observed as a holiday in Greece for all educational establishments; commemorative services are held and students attend school only for these, while some schools and all universities stay closed during the day. Here on Skopelos, students honour the tradition by having a holiday after the services and 'cocking a snook' at authority - under the indulgent eyes of the townspeople. Since 1973, police, armed forces or anyone in politics are not allowed onto educational premises without permission. Pupils have been known to lock out their teachers by padlocking the doors to the school. When this happens, the school remains closed until pupils relent!

December 6th - The feast of **Ayios Nikolaos** (Saint Nicholas), the patron of seafarers, who has many churches and chapels dedicated to him on the island.

December 25th - A much less festive occasion than Greek Easter, **Christmas** (*Khristouyenna*) is still an important religious feast celebrating the birth of Christ, and in recent years it has started to take on more of the trappings of the western Christmas, with decorations, Christmas trees and gifts.

December 26th **– Synaxis tis Panayias** is the gathering of the Virgin's Entourage.

Beautiful whitewashed churches on the headland below the Kastro, Skopelos Town

Culture and Tradition

Childbirth

There are many traditions, customs and superstitions surrounding children and childbirth. Here are but a few:

When a child is born, a name is not given immediately; the child is not officially named until the baptism.

For the first forty days after the birth of the child, no visitors are allowed into the house. After this, until the baptism, the child can only be visited in the day – never in the night. This is due to the fact that the child has not yet been blessed by the Church and is therefore unable to ward off evil spirits.

The mother must not go out in the night at all and no clothes of anyone inside the household, but particularly the mother and child, must be hung outside in the night, lest the spirits use this as a means to getting inside the house. The spirits' intention is to corrupt the child with bad feelings and give him a 'bad heart'.

When people come to visit, they sometimes leave coins under the baby's or mother's pillow to bring good luck and fortune. For families who are strictly Orthodox, the baptism will take place immediately after the 40 day period, but generally now, the baptism will take place anywhere between the child's first and second years.

Until it has been baptised, the child is only referred to as 'Baby'. The baby is given a name in the baptismal service. If it is the first child born to the grandparents, it normally takes the grandfather's name if a boy; or grandmother's if a girl. There are no middle names as such, unless the child is born on the day of an Orthodox Saint. Should this be the case and it is the first grandchild, two names may be given - that of the Saint and another. If it is not the first grandchild, only the Saint's name will be given as this is seen as a very good omen for the child.

Engagements

Although Western culture, particularly with the advent of the European Union, is impacting on the culture of Greece, the old traditions, especially in small or more remote towns and villages, still exist.

Quite often two families will discuss their respective offspring as potential partners for each other and in fact introduce them to each other. They will then be allowed to get to know each other to see if they are compatible and if there is sufficient affection for the relationship to develop into something further. If this is the case, the couple will continue to court until such a time as they decide that the girls' family be approached by the boy to ask for their daughter's hand in marriage.

If they agree, then the couple will make a verbal contract to be engaged and married. Although this is not always the case and a lot of couples just meet and choose each other as they do in western societies, in some villages the purpose of the marriage may well be not for love, but for a sound business proposition.

In major towns you will often see many older men with younger wives— older men are considered more secure financially. In rural communities it is more important that the man be young and strong. When the details of the marriage contract are settled between the couples' fathers, and rings have been exchanged, the bride's father gives the groom's father a tray of basil for good luck. Then he hands his future son-in-law a glass of coins to signify that he will now support and provide for his bride.

The engagement is far more important than the actual wedding itself. This is the personal commitment that the couple make to each other. From now on, they refer to each other as husband and wife. To end an engagement is the same as a divorce and can be seen as shameful by the families concerned.

On Skopelos, the traditional engagement dress, now no longer worn, but seen on occasions at festivals, is distinguished from other traditional costumes by its very broad green border.

Marriage

Marriage is celebrated through the rite of *crowning*, showing the importance of eternal union of the couple. Although marriage is seen as a permanent commitment in life and in death, remarriage and divorce are permitted in certain circumstances.

The wedding ceremony is a public affirmation of the commitment the couple made to each other at their engagement. It is a joyful affair, celebrated by the whole community and often, on the mainland, involving a thousand guests. Here on Skopelos, we have no Aphrodite's Palace – a large, purpose built place in which to hold weddings where the guests are invited in such numbers - so large numbers are invited to the church and a few families only go to the reception.

Traditional Wedding Rituals

Weddings in Greece are full of rich religious symbolism, exuberant dancing, and of course, great food. The seven days leading up to a Greek wedding are full of rituals and fun and the bride's girlfriends or bridesmaids play an important part in the run up to the ceremony.

The Nuptial Flag

Greek wedding preparations begin on the Monday before the typical Sunday wedding. The first step, traditionally, was the preparation of the flamboro; a nuptial 'flag' displayed outside the bride's house. To make the flamboro, her bridesmaids would find a long branch that ended in five twigs. An apple tied to one of the twigs symbolised love and maternity, tufts of red wool on the other four twigs symbolised household thrift and industry. Nowadays the flamboro is more likely to be swathes of net, tulle or lace around the balconies and railings of the house. Once the flamboro is finished, the wedding festivities begin.

Hiding the Ring

On the Wednesday night before the wedding, the bride's mother and the bridesmaids bake breads and wedding cakes while relatives and friends watch. As the women begin sifting the flour they toss coins into a sieve and shout 'Kalorizika! Kalorizika!' which means 'Good luck! Good luck!'. Relatives pull pieces of dough from the mixing bowl and daub the faces of the groom and bride with it. While the crowd is distracted by this, a young girl hides a wedding ring and coins in the dough. Friends and family continue to party at the bride's house until dawn, with plenty of singing, dancing, drinking and sometimes even rifle firing.

Finding the Ring

On Thursday, the women gather again. They section off the dough they made the day before and each takes a portion of the mixture. They then look for the ring and coins smuggled in by the young girl. The lucky finder of the ring presents it to the groom and gets a gift in return.

Breaking the Cake

Once the dough is returned to the mixing trough, the women begin to bake the 'propkasto', the largest of the wedding cakes. Once it is done, the groom puts the cake over a bowl of water; grabs the bride's friends and dances around it three times singing the wedding cake song. Then the bridesmaids and the groomsmen break the cake into pieces and shower the couple with it. They also throw a quilt over the couple as an additional symbol of abundance and fertility.

Filling the Dowry Sacks

On the Friday before the big day, the bridesmaids arrive at the bride's home, bringing her rice and cotton for good luck. On this day the bride packs up her things for her new life. A Greek mother will start preparing for this day from very early on in her daughter's life, sewing and weaving a beautiful collection of quilts and other bed linen, tablecloths, blankets, wall tapestries and many other things. The collections can be enormous, very beautiful and of course every stitch is hand woven with a mother's love! The bride's mother starts the packing by putting a large copper saucepan in a homespun sack (these days boxes or suitcases provide an easier way to start things!) then the bride packs up her 'bottom drawer and clothes'. When all is packed, the bridesmaids sprinkle all the bags with rice and herbs. Then women begin making traditional dishes like loaves of bread inscribed with symbolic dough patterns.

The Dressing Dance

On the wedding day, friends and relatives go to the bride's home to dance in the courtyard while the bride dresses. They form a circle and dance traditional syrtaki dances. The dancing creates a lively atmosphere and continues until the late afternoon or until the procession begins.

The Best Man

No one is as busy or is as important (save the bride and groom) at an Orthodox wedding, than the Best Man or 'Koumbaros' as he is known. Often, he bears the main cost of the wedding celebration. It is not unusual to have several 'best men' in order to spread these costs. After the wedding he remains an important figure in the couple's life, eventually becoming Godfather to their first child.

On the morning of the wedding, the groom's male friends, the 'vratimi', set out to collect the 'koumbaros'. They used to hoist a white flag decorated with apples and herbs outside his house, before escorting him to the groom's house.

He must bring with him two large white candles tied in a bouquet of orange blossoms. They will be used in the traditional Orthodox Joining Ceremony.

Led by the 'koumbaros', the groom then leaves his house, and goes to the bride's family home.

Blessing the Groom

Traditionally, the groom would ride to the bride's house on horseback accompanied by music, shouts and gunfire – these days he arrives in the most expensive car available to him!

He is greeted by his future mother-in law at the door. She offers him some wine, a ring of shaped biscuit and a boutonniere of spices and herbs wrapped in a white handkerchief. He pins this to his lapel, kisses her hand and asks for her blessing. She gives her blessing by kissing her future son-in-law on both cheeks. She may also touch his neck with incense and give him 'embatikion', a gift symbolising that he has joined the family.

Serenading the Bride

As the groomsmen load the bride's things in the wedding car, her mother puts a piece of raw cotton in each dowry sack (or suitcase) - a symbolic blessing that the marriage will be prosperous. When the couple arrive at the threshold of the groom's house, her bridesmaids will serenade the bride with a song about the Greek goddess of Hymen, to symbolise that her time as a virgin has passed.

The Bridal Party

Traditionally the wedding took place at the groom's house and the 'vratimi' loaded the Bride's dowry into the groom's carriage for the journey. They used to fire their guns to ward away evil spirits. During the journey, the vratimi would bless the couple by showering them with cottonseed, rice, small coins and flower petals. Today, once the bride's father has agreed to the marriage, the couple follow their 'koumbaros' to the Church, accompanied by musicians, singing and dancing.

The Wedding Ceremony

As the honoured director of the ceremony, the 'koumbaros' leads the ring exchanging ceremony. The most important moment of the ceremony is the placing of the Crowns on the couples' heads. The crowns are always very beautiful and elaborate, made of silver, sometimes with flowers and pearls intricately woven into them. Traditionally, the crowns were woven with orange blossoms, sometimes interspersed with olive leaves. The 'koumbaros' swaps the wedding bands back and forth between the couple's heads three times, to signify the Holy Trinity.

The crowns can be said to symbolise many things. Most believe that it crowns the couple as King and Queen of their own little kingdom, their home. Others say that it evokes the crown of thorns worn by Jesus and others that it signifies the couples' triumph over passion and is a reward for their virtue.

The crowns are joined together by a ribbon, symbolising the unity of the couple forever from this moment forth. After the ceremony, the crowns are removed and placed on the altar.

Following the exchange of the rings, during which the wedding bands are placed on the right hand, sometimes the couple are given candles to hold for the remainder of the ceremony as a symbol of their willingness to receive God's blessings.

The priest also joins the couples' right hands together whilst praying for their marriage. The Bride and Groom continue to hold hands throughout the remainder of the ceremony as a symbol of their union.

No vows are exchanged during the ceremony, in fact the couple do not speak at all because marriage is not considered a contract but a union of two people in love.

After the priest reads the bible passages, the Bride and Groom take three sips of wine from a shared cup. The ritual of the common cup is based on the wedding of Canaan in Galilee, where Jesus turned water into wine. The cup represents life and symbolises the couple's mutual sharing of joy and sorrow.

As they drink wine from the common cup, they are reminded that from that moment they will share everything, doubling their joys and dividing their sorrows.

The priest, the groom, the bride and the 'koumbaros' join hands and make three circles around the altar, stopping after each quarter turn, so that guests can shower them with good wishes in the form of rice, flowers and sugared almonds. This is called the 'march of Isaiah' and they are the first steps the couple make together into their new life together.

Walnuts

In some places on Skopelos, the wedding ceremony will end with honey and walnuts offered to the bride and groom from silver spoons. Walnuts are chosen because they break into four parts; symbolising the bride, the groom, and the two sets of family.

Sugar Coated Almonds

In traditional Greek weddings, 'koufetta' (almonds) are placed in odd numbers in little bags. The fresh almonds have a bittersweet taste, reminding us that life is both bitter and sweet. The sugar coating is added in the hope that the life of the newlyweds will have more sweetness than bitterness. The odd number is indivisible, symbolising how the husband and wife will share everything and remain undivided. The 'koufetta' are also carried to guests on a silver tray.

The belief holds that if an unmarried woman takes them off the tray and puts them under her pillow, she will dream that night of the man that she will marry.

Breaking the Plates

The old custom of breaking the plates still takes place, at the reception. A member of the immediate family, usually the mother or the sister, begins the destruction by throwing a plate on the dance floor. Others follow suit. The broken plates symbolise good luck and happiness and the permanence of Marriage. The immediate family of the bride pin money to the bride's dress for luck, good fortune and prosperity.

Greek Orthodox weddings cannot be performed during periods of fasting, after Easter and Christmas and the day preceding a holy day.

Funerals

Greeks mourn and show respect for their dead for a long time after they have departed this world. When somebody dies, it depends somewhat on the time of the day that they die as to the ritual that ensues. Close relatives living in the same house as the dead person must stay up with the body all night or for up to 24 hours. Friends and relatives come round to the house, nobody sleeps and they will make company together on this, the last night on this earth of the departed.

In the room in the house where the body is kept, nothing in the way of food or drink must be served. No meat is eaten at all for 9 days by anybody in the household as they believe that the body is not yet dead. Flesh represents the flesh of Christ and all things living and the abstinence from eating meat is a mark of respect, until the person properly departs this world. The body, particularly the face, is covered with a sheet as soon as the sun goes down, and is not uncovered until the sun rises. This has to do with evil spirits that may corrupt the soul in the night. The body must be placed in the middle of the room where it is kept, facing the direction of the sunrise.

After the 24 hour or night vigil, everybody goes to the Church, the dead body leading the procession and everyone following. The coffin is open during the procession for all to see and then for one hour in the church to give people a chance to pay their last respects, whilst the priests read from the Bible.

The body is always buried with the other family members, on top of the previous member's grave. A daughter who has been married will be buried with her husband's family, as she becomes part of that family when she marries him. The family looks after the grave as if it is the new home of the departed, keeping it clean at all times and laying fresh flowers regularly. Sometimes candles will be lit.

After nine days, the family makes a special plate called 'koliva'. This consists of raisins, wheat and walnuts and is displayed inside the house and then taken to the grave, as food for the dead. The priests attend and give readings. Part of the food is scattered over the grave and the relatives eat the remainder. This is a mark of respect and acknowledgment that the dead person is still part of the family and can still eat with them.

After 40 days, normally the nearest Sunday mass, another plate of 'koliva' is made and taken to the church. It is passed around the congregation in the church and everybody eats from the plate. The same ritual is performed after 6 months and then again after 1 year as the Greeks believe it can sometimes take this long for the body to ascend to God. Some families will repeat the ritual again after 3 years.

The wearing of black as a mark of respect depends on how close the family members were to the deceased. For the immediate family, black is worn by women for 1 year. If a husband dies, the wife is supposed to wear black forever to respect her husband, unless she is young enough to marry again one day. Otherwise, the wife is expected to grieve for the remainder of her life. The only time she may go away from black is if she attends family weddings or baptisms, as black is bad luck at these joyous occasions. Then she may wear grey or dark blue instead. If a wife or female member of the family dies, the husband or relative wears a black armband. In some villages, a black material is hung over the doorway of the house to show that someone has recently died. Many men on Skopelos follow the tradition of not shaving for 40 days after the death and 40 days after each of the other landmark rituals.

Funerals must take place within 24 hours because of the climate and the fact that there are no refrigeration facilities on the island. The cemetery is situated on the old road to Raches, which is off the ring road. The dead are buried with their heads pointing east, so that they will be able to witness the angel's trumpet blast to signal the Second Coming of Christ.

Unless it is an old family plot, the burial site is only rented from the church. After a period of time (not less than 3 years), the body is exhumed, washed with rose water and certain bones (the skull and long bones) are placed in a casket in the ossuary or taken to the family land for reburial. There is an ossuary at the Monastery of Taxiarchos near Glossa.

The traditional dress of Skopelos

Greek stories of gods, heroes and monsters are told and retold around the world even today. The earliest known versions of myths and legends date back more than 2,700 years, appearing in written form in the works of the Greek poets Homer and Hesiod. But some of these myths are much older. Indeed, the Greeks borrowed some of their best material from other, more ancient traditions.

Skopelos has managed to maintain much of its unique cultural foundation, its legends and rich traditions, despite the destruction of many of its historic and artistic monuments, castles and monasteries. As is the case throughout Greece, it is astonishing how myths and reality get interwoven in a unique way and the story of the patron saint of Skopelos illustrates this.

The following myths and legends are supposedly Skopelos based: as for their true foundation - who knows?

The Alkyon Myth

Alkyon was one of the seven daughters of Aeolos, god of the winds. Her husband was king Ceynx, who in turn was the son of the deity Eosphorus (Hesperius). Ceynx was very content with his life and his wife, and decided this happiness was reason enough for him to call his wife Hera. He also made Alkyon call him Zeus. This, of course, incited the wrath of the gods, and they were changed into birds as a punishment.

According to another myth, Ceynx drowned in a shipwreck during a trip to consult an oracle. Alkyon was so much in love with her husband that when she heard of his death she jumped from a cliff, so that they could be together for all eternity. The gods took pity on them, and transformed them into sea birds. Alkyon was turned into a Kingfisher, or Halcyon, and Ceynx into a Gannet, or Ceyx.

The Kingfisher has its nesting period during the winter solstice. Alkyon's father, Aeolos, ensures that the winds don't blow and the weather is warm for some days after the 15th January when the eggs of these birds hatch. If you are lucky, you will see these birds on the shore at Stafilos, as well as other places around the island.

During the winter months when the weather is calm for a few days, the Greeks say we have 'Halcyon days'. The people of Skopelos expect fifteen of these days in January - and they usually get them!

The Dragon Myth

Long ago on the island of Skopelos there lived a fierce dragon which was attacking the islanders and eating them. The people were so frightened that they fled the island, leaving it deserted.

The rulers of Greece decided that the dragon was a good way to execute criminals, so they dispatched them by ship to Panormos and an unnamed port now called Elios. The dragon duly obliged and each shipload of prisoners was eaten by the time the next one arrived. This went on for 400 years.

Then a man called Righinos decided to put an end to the killing. He was hired as a deckhand on the prison ship. When the boat landed at the unnamed port, he leapt ashore, brandishing a sword and shouting, 'Where in the name of mercy is the dragon?' The Greek word for mercy is 'elios' and the port was given this name, which it still bears today.

He fought the dragon all the way along the coast , until finally the dragon was brought to bay at the edge of the sea between Stafilos and Agnontas. Righinos slew the dragon and the strength of his righteous arm cut a huge schism into the rock, into which the dragon fell. Rejoicing, the inhabitants returned to the island, which Righinos made his home.

Dragon's Schism can be found on the road about 1.5 km past Stafilos, on the second dirt track on the left. It is a beautiful spot high above the sea, marked with a small shrine dedicated to Righinos.

It is unclear if this Righinos is the same person as the saint, although he is depicted as such.

The Lady of the Lake

Skopelos has always been a place full of running waters. This is why this island is so fertile. There are two high mountains (Palouki and Delfi) full of streams, springs and... fairies. On the mainland there is a stream that sustains water all year round. It is called Limni (Lake) and this is where the fairies came from. They came to Skopelos and bathed in the streams each midnight, when no one would be passing by.

One night, almost one hundred years ago, a drunken man, who had lost his way from the taverna to his house, passed by the stream and heard voices and singing. He had heard the stories about the fairies, but never thought that he would actually see them.

Hidden behind a bush, he saw the fairies bathing in the crystal clear waters of the stream, under the light of the full moon. Dazzled, he stood there and watched them. Then he suddenly realized that he was standing next to where the fairies had left their clothes. Before the fairies could see him, he grabbed a scarf belonging to one of them and hid.

But the fairies saw him and they all ran away, as all fairies do when they see a man. All but the one who couldn't find her scarf. That was the only way to catch a fairy; you had to steal her scarf.

So the man took the fairy with him and soon they got married. They lived happily and had two beautiful children. The man had given up his drinking and he worked in the fields from dawn till dusk, so as to provide his family with everything they needed. No one in the village knew his wife's secret.

One day the fairy was looking for some old clothes to quilt and she found her scarf! She put it on and disappeared. Everyone was searching for the man's wife but couldn't find her, so they all said that she was lost and gone.

However, when the man came home every night he would find the house clean and tidy and the children fed and food cooked. The beautiful fairy loved her husband and children very much and so she would come every morning to do the housework and then disappear.

One day however, the man stayed at home in the morning and when he saw the fairy, he took her scarf and threw it in the fire. So the fairy stayed with her husband forever. And they lived happily ever after.

The dolls to be found hanging on the walls of many tourist shops, with long hair and dresses, are representations of these fairies or nymphs of the waters.

The Legend of Adrina

In 1276 the Knight Licario, commander of the Byzantine fleet, took over Skopelos and drove out the Venetians. A long time of pirate raids began for the island. The pirates used it for their anchor point since it was in the perfect place for raids; ships sailing from the port of Thessaloniki and headed south would pass either through the passage between Skopelos and Alonnisos or east between Skiathos and Skopelos.

Panormos and Blo, which means 'sheltered harbour', were ideal places to protect the sailors from the wind. This is where the pirates anchored their ships. Among them was the pirate woman Adrina, the terror of the northern Aegean sea and the only female pirate that sailed the Greek seas.

Adrina and her companion had just stolen a Venetian ship full of gold. So they sailed to Blo and got ready to celebrate, as they usually did after a good raid. The pirates went to Skopelos to bring food and wine. Adrina stayed in the port alone to guard the ship and make sure no local would come near.

The pirates made their way up to Mourtero, passed Alikias and the river and finally arrived at the little church of Holy Mary the Fighter. It is a small church which can still be seen today, built on the hill of Pefkia.

The locals were having a feast and at the time were dancing there. The pirates joined the dance and started singing a strange song. The locals that were not too drunk heard the song and as soon as they understood its meaning they ran away. The slaughter of the rest did not take long to begin. But as soon as the first local dropped dead, the Virgin Mary appeared with her sword and those that had enough courage left chased the pirates until they had slaughtered them all.

As soon as Adrina found out what had happened to her men, she took the treasure from the ship and sank it in Blo. It took her hours to hide the treasure and when she finished, she climbed on a rock near Panormos and fell into the sea. The place has been called Adrina since then.

It is said that her treasure is very large. It included a golden pig with her piglets, and many local people are still trying to find it...

The Legend of Chadoula

We owe most of the historical data, referring to the last 5 centuries (1400 – 1900) about the Sporades, to various explorers and geographers. They left us a priceless heritage. A great collection of texts from geographers and travellers, from 15th until the 19th century, was compiled in 1997 by Adamantios Samson of Skopelos. His book can be found in the folk art museum of Skopelos.

This translation from his book '**Wanderers and Geographers of North Sporades**' is the report of an English wanderer named Bernard Randolph, dated 1687:

"At the north side of Skopelos is a large port named Porto Palerma, where the Venetians often come. Here stands a high castle that defended the port from the Venetians for a short period, but in the end the locals had to surrender and pay an annual fee in order to keep their privileges and not be obliged to ask for a military guard from them. Here live many merchants that have commercial affairs with Cairo and other places…"

At that time, a very rich merchant lived in Skopelos. He owned many ships that sailed the Mediterranean and he had a daughter named Chadoula; a beautiful girl, and raised like a princess. In their mansion, which was the biggest in Skopelos, one could find gold, silk, amber, mastic, myrrh and incense. Many men were in love with her, but she was in love with a young nobleman from Glossa. The young man asked her father to allow them to marry. Her father accepted with joy and they were engaged.

Skiathos was pillaged by the Turkish admiral Morozinis in 1660 and he now turned to Skopelos, intending to pillage there as well. The locals had fought hard against many other enemies in the past. The bravest men of the island, including Chadoula's husband, boarded three ships and sailed to fight the enemy.

"Do not be afraid", said the man to Chadoula. "Rest assured that I will return as a winner. But should I die in battle you shall know it, for my men will leave our black sails on our ships, instead of changing them for sails of victory".

Chadoula waited for days in agony, until finally she saw the ships returning - with their black sails up! In despair, she flung herself into the sea to drown. As her body hit the water, she turned into a rock. The tragic irony was that her husband was still alive. They had won the battle and in their excitement had forgotten to change the sails.

Upon arriving to Skopelos from the west, you can't miss Chadoula. It is the big rock in the middle of the sea just in front of the kastro.

Icon Myths

When Constantinople was invaded by the Turks, in order to prevent the church icons from being burnt and destroyed, the monks threw them into the sea. It is believed that they were then carried by the currents and winds to the shores of Greek islands and the mainland over the centuries.

Because Skopelos is populated on its north coast facing Constantinople, many of these icons were found here.

The monasteries and churches of Evangelistra, Ag. Ioannis Kastri and Panagia Livadiotisa are all built on the sites where miraculously appearing icons were discovered (see Monasteries and Churches sections).

View along the rugged north east coast

Monasteries

Mount Athos is a mountain and a peninsula in Macedonia, northern Greece, called Άγιο Όρος (Ayion Oros or 'Holy Mountain') in Modern Greek. It is described as the centre of Orthodox Monasticism. The Holy Mount is a self-governed part of the Greek state, subject to the Ministry of Foreign Affairs in its political aspect. Skopelos is over 50 miles away from Mount Athos, but its presence can usually be detected on the horizon if you stand on the Kastro. A clear view from the island is thought to be lucky.

In order to reduce sexual temptation, women are completely barred from the peninsula, a fact which has earned a certain amount of fame; even female domestic animals (with the exception, some say, of cats, as well as chickens which lay eggs that provide the fresh egg yolk needed for the paint used in iconography) are forbidden. However, during the Greek Civil War, Athos did shelter refugees including women and girls. Visits to the peninsula are possible for laymen, but they need special permission.

Monasteries on Skopelos

There are several monasteries on Skopelos, most of them high up and offering fantastic views over the island.

Zoodochos Pigi

This monastery, to be seen up the steps at the end of the old harbour, is one of the many monasteries located in Skopelos Town. It was built in the 18th century and belongs to the monastery Xiropotamou of Mount Athos. Zoodochos is a Greek term meaning 'life-receiving'. The monastery of Zoodochos Pigi translates literally as 'the source of life'.

It has a superb 18th century church called Panaghia Eleftherotria (the liberating Virgin), which has a slate roof with brightly painted ceramics on it and a fountain hidden behind a huge plane tree. There are also rare Byzantine icons and beautiful frescoes.

The church of Agia Varvara has a cross-like dome and a beautiful, wooden temple with three gates: one dedicated to Agia Varvara, the second to the Circumcision of the Christ and the third to Agios Charalambosis . Inside the church, there is a miraculous icon reputedly painted by Saint Luke the

Evangelist, who, according to legend, painted the first icons that ever existed. The icon is extremely old and the people of Skopelos are under pressure to allow it to be taken to the icon museum of Athens.

Episkopi (Bishopric)

The monastery of Episkopi is one of the few Venetian monasteries to have survived, partially, from the Ottoman invasion. It is located west of Skopelos Town, on the left hand turn off to Ag. Righinos, after the medical centre. Almost immediately after the turn, you will see the Episkopi on your right, with its high rising stone walls, three buttresses and long narrow windows. The stone supports of a balcony that was never built can be seen, with their ends sculptured into the images of animals. The building is Venetian and was never completed. It is assumed that the building activities were disrupted when the island was ransacked by the Turk Chairedin Babarossa in 1538.

In the courtyard of the Episkopi is the single aisle basilica of Panagia tis Episkopis, honoured on August 23rd. On the eve a vigil is held, followed by a service on the next day, which is attended by the whole town. The church is used by the community for weddings and baptisms. It dates back to the 17th century and has wall inscriptions and one old relief. The iconostasis dates from between the 17th and 18th centuries.

The building stands on the site of an earlier church, commissioned in 1078 by Bishop Anastasios and an even older Early Christian church, dating back to 600 AD. This is also the site of an ancient Temple of Athene or of Artemis. The ground level buildings with their tower on the right were constructed between the end of the 17th and 19th centuries. The buildings of the Episkopi have been completely renovated and the work was finished in 1964. This valuable historical project is maintained and financed solely by the owners.

Panaghia Livadiotissa

This monastery, dedicated to the Virgin Mary of the Meadow, is located 2 kilometres from Skopelos Town on the Spitalia road skirting the bay beyond the port. Immediately before the site of the ancient Temple of Asklepios, (see Archaeological Sites section) turn up the road on the right. Fifty metres further on, in the olive groves on the right, is the uninhabited monastery of Panaghia Livadiostissa. It stands in the area of Ambeliki and in the past belonged to the monastery of Ag. Ekaterina of Sina.

The monastery was built during the 17th century and houses some very interesting icons one of which, an icon of 1671 by the Cretan painter A. Agorastos, is said to be miraculous.

About 350 years ago, locals saw a bright light in the bay. On investigation, they found an icon in the sea, and decided to build a church on the site. They began, but next day discovered the building knocked down and the icon missing. They found the icon in the dunes in the place where the church stands today. This is considered to be a miracle, as the original location for the church is now, because of erosion, under the sea.

Aghios Righinos

The church was built in 1728 on the site of older places of worship. It was a Byzantine building, a one room basilica with dome, that was demolished in order to build a big cross-shaped cathedral type church. Behind the monastery are the remains of a Doric temple.

In the western part of the monastery is the 4th century stone sarcophagus of Righinos, the bishop of Skopelos, who died as a martyr in 362 AD. He is commemorated on February 25th (see Saints' days and holidays).

On the eve of the day there is a service held at Christos, where the remains of the Saint are held. The following day the townspeople make a procession from Christos to the monastery, taking the holy relics with them. They attend a service and afterwards return the relics to Christos. A commemorative service is also held at the Palio Ghiofiri, the small shrine at the T junction opposite the restaurant 'Nastas.' This is the site of the Saint's execution.

Evangelistra

Four kilometres from Skopelos town, on the far side of the bay, this 18th century monastery is located in a very beautiful place, offering one of the most magnificent views of the Town nestling in the bay and the hills opposite, with Mount Delfi towering over all.

The monastery is that of the Annunciation, built in 1712 by Stephanos Dhapontes, the English ambassador, on the site of an older monastery founded by monks from Mount Athos. The earlier monastery was related to Constantinople, where a holy cross with a portrait of 'Panagia Pamakaristos' (Virgin Mary) was implanted. According to the tradition this was brought to the island by two monks who came from Constantinople during the reign of Nikiforos Fokas (963-969).

Dhapontes decided to restore the monastery at his own expense, because of a miracle of Panagia (Virgin Mary) which saved him when he was sent to the island's Turkish ruler, the Aga, to be put to death. It now belongs to the Monastery of Xiropotamos of Athos.

It has a huge, impressive gold plated 14th century altar screen from Constantinople, as well as very interesting and valuable icons. Only one monk is in residence now, and he is looked after by several elderly nuns. The nuns make and sell textiles and other handicrafts in a small shop beside the church.

There is also a small chapel in the monastery which is dedicated to the protector of the sailors, Saint Nikolaos.

Agia Varvara

The Monastery of Agia Varvara (St. Barbara) is found about 6km to the North of Skopelos Town, close to the Monastery of Agios Ioannis. It is abandoned today, but used to have an important role for the island till some decades ago.

The Monastery was founded in 1648 and it was reformed in 1697. The architecture of this Monastery looks like a fortress: a tall, stone wall surrounds the church and the yard. Its location actually overlooks the sea, so it may have been used as a lookout post for enemies and pirates in previous centuries. It now belongs to the Local Authority of Skopelos and is used on occasion for public performances. A caretaker is employed to open the monastery to visitors in the summer.

Ag. Varvara is the patron saint of artillerymen, military engineers, miners and others who work with explosives, because of her legend's association with lightning.

On December 4th, her saint's day, a panayiri takes place at the monastery.

Prodromos

This convent is dedicated to Saint John the Baptist and was built during the 18th century, on the top of a hill, visible from the Monastery of Metamorphosis. It was renovated by the monk Filaretos and has a beautiful iconostasis. It is also the custodian of many documents dating back to the

Turkish occupation and fine icons dating from the 16th, 17th and 18th centuries. The monastery was originally male, but in the 1920's was taken over by women. It is now inhabited by a few nuns and only opened during its feast day.

Metamorfosis

This 16th century monastery is called the Monastery of the Transfiguration and is surrounded by a clutch of pines. It has a small beautiful chapel standing in a flowered courtyard, within which are the obligatory beautiful iconostasis, old vestments, rare books and holy relics. It is opened on its feast day, the 6th of August, during which one of the biggest festivals of the island takes place (See Festivals and celebrations section).

Taxiarches

The Taxiarches Monastery is located opposite the monastery of Ag. Anna. Both monasteries are now abandoned. The Monastery of Taxiarches is well hidden out of sight by overgrown plane and walnut trees.

Tradition states that on the east side of Palouki mountain the people of Skopelos began to build the monastery of Taxiarches in a place called Vatos, some 200 years ago. But when the walls reached the first metre in height, the construction could not be completed! The builders would still build, but in a strange way the walls would not get any higher. As if this wasn't enough, every night the walls would move by themselves, and would set themselves in another place that was southeast and half an hour further away. Finally the builders gave in and managed to finish the monastery on its new site, leaving the first building half finished.

The nearby mountain caves are used as goat pens and there is a spring. During the Second World War, the partisans hid British, New Zealand and Greek soldiers here in the monastery, before helping them to escape to Turkey and the Middle East.

Aghios Ioannis Kastri (Mamma Mia! Church)

On the northern coast of Skopelos is a small island, formed when part of the cliff fell into the sea. The villagers have built a small chapel and christened it with the name 'Ag. John the Beheaded', or John the Baptist.

Just before reaching Glossa, take the signposted road on the right and follow it, ignoring the immediate right hand fork. Continue on the road, past the three scarecrows, whose purpose is a mystery, until you come to the church of Panagia, from where there are superb views of the coastline including Ag. Ioannis. After this visit, the road winds down to the base of Ag. Ioannis, perched on a precipitous rock above.

The legend says that while some fishermen were working on their boats on the beaches next to the sheer rock, they saw a bright light glowing in the sea. They went to investigate and found in the water an icon of Ag. Ioannis. Leaving it on the beach, the fishermen returned next day to find it missing, only to discover it once more on top of the rock next to a lighted candle. This became the site of the small monastery that exists today. It was built using nets and pulleys reminiscent of the monasteries at Meteora.

Every year on the 29th August, Mass is celebrated in the chapel to commemorate the life of St. John the Baptist. The inside of the chapel is very small and is not the one featured in the film 'Mamma Mia!', which was rebuilt in Pinewood Studios following the designs of the small church Panagitsa tou Pirgou located on Skopelos harbour.

There are 200 steps to the church, up which Meryl Streep ran without stopping (incredibly, the scene was canned in only one take!) after singing 'The Winner Takes It All' to Sam. Inside the chapel there is a visitors' book which you can sign if you wish.

Agia Varvara, the fortified monastery on Mount Palouki

Churches

The island of Skopelos has more than 360 churches and chapels. Most are closed through the year except for the feast day of whom or to whatever the church has been dedicated. Most have been privately built. The oldest existing ecclesiastical structure is the basilica of Agios Athanasios built in the 11th century and located in the Kastro area. All except one of the churches on the island observe the Greek Orthodox faith. The remaining church hosts a small enclave of Jehovah's Witnesses.

Christianity was formalized in Skopelos by the appointment of the Bishop Righinos in the 4th Century A.D. Under the reign of the Emperor Julian the Apostate, Righinos was martyred in 362 A.D. The Saint's feast day is February 25th - a holiday on the island.

There are five main churches in Skopelos town and the three priests rotate between them. It is customary for the congregations to follow their priest on the days when their own churches are closed for services, which are announced by the tolling of the bell three times. A sequence of two tolls of the bell denotes a funeral or commemorative funeral service.

Glossa and Elios, of course, have their own churches, the most prominent being churches to Aghios Nicolaos, the patron saint of sailors.

If you are interested in visiting any of the churches in Skopelos, please read the section on church etiquette.

Church Etiquette

Anyone may visit a church, even during a service, as long as they are appropriately dressed (shoulders and legs covered) and behave respectfully.

Should you see Greeks waiting outside the church, you must wait also. It is considered to be very bad manners to enter the church when the pappas is holding the chalice, so the people will be waiting for that part of the service to be over. They will tell you when to enter. It is the proper custom to be at Church for the beginning of the Liturgy or at least before the Epistle and Gospel Readings.

Churches of Skopelos

There are many, many churches on Skopelos. Below are cited only the main churches which hold services regularly throughout the year, and have their own, or share, a priest.

Church of Panaghia ston Pirgho (Panagitsa)

This church is located in Skopelos Town and is the most famous church of Skopelos, appearing on many postcards as an iconic Greek motif, along with the windmills of Mykonos, and the blue-domed churches of Santorini. The inside of this church was the model for Sky and Sophia's wedding chapel in the film 'Mamma Mia!', reconstructed at Pinewood.

Panagia Papameletiou (Kimissis tis Theotokou)

This church was built between 1662-68, but the entrance is more modern. The original church was built in the shape of the cross. The iconostasis was made by the famous Cretan master craftsman Antonios Aghorastos. It was transferred here from the monastery tou Stavrou, which collapsed during the earthquake of 1965. The four one-piece columns, which support the dome, are different in size and colour. It is likely that they originated from older Byzantine churches.

Aghios Nikolaou

Agios Nikolaou, 'victory of the people', is the common name for **Nicholas of Myra**, a saint and Bishop of Myra (in Lycia, part of modern-day Turkey). This is the state basilica. It is to be found just off the Paralea up the main shopping street. Aghios Nicholaou is the patron saint of sailors, merchants, archers, students and children in Greece. Because of the many miracles attributed to his intercession, he is also known as Nicholas the Wonderworker. He had a reputation for secret gift-giving, such as putting coins in the shoes of those who left them out for him, and thus became the model for Santa Claus, whose English name comes from the Dutch Sinterklaas. The church was recently renovated and has some interesting old icons and a Holy Virgin sculptured in marble.

The Church of Genesis tou Christo (sto Christo)

This, the church of the nativity of Christ, is one of the most important churches in town and has a checkered history. It is the one with the elaborate bell tower. The belfry has parts which come from an older Byzantine church. The bell was presented to Skopelos by the Russian admiral leading the Greek fleet, in thanks for the efforts of Skopeliti sailors in destroying the Turkish fleet in the War of Independence. The iconostasis dates from 1765, but the church was built later. In front of the altar there is a marble plaque with Armenian inscription. It has a special arrangement of the apse, which is a half hexagon, instead of the more usual half spherical shape. In the church there are vaults in which former bishops of Skopelos are buried.

Panagia Faneromeni

This church, that of 'the appeared virgin', (Faneromeni) is situated opposite the nursery school. This particular icon of the Virgin Mary usually depicts her with the Christ Child on her knee, and has the nickname 'the virgin of the sweet kisses'. There is usually a festival to Faneromeni held in mid August every year.

Built at the beginning of the 18th century in 1711, the church of Panagia Faneromeni was first used as a monastery dependent on the monastery of Agios Dionysios of Mount Athos. The walls of the building contain columns from ancient classical buildings and a tomb relief. The church has a clock tower, which chimes the hours and half hours.

From Platanos Square, go up the hill through town and take the second turning on the left. Go up the steps and turn right, then follow the building round to the entrance. There is a large flat terrace beside the church.

Aghios Nikolaos Loutraki

This church is situated by the harbour side at Loutraki, to the right as you walk towards the fish tavernas. It is dedicated to Aghios Nikolaos, the patron saint of sailors, and has a separate campanile. It is very simple in style, but has a peaceful serenity.

Panagia Eleftherotria Glossa

This is an eighteenth century church built during the Turkish occupation and, like most of the houses of Glossa, this is reflected in its architecture, being built in the Macedonian style. Found high above the town, it has breathtaking views. Its name is derived from the Greek Anthem: **Eleftheria** i Thanatos (Liberty or Death).

Kimissis Theodokou Glossa

The church to the Dormition of the Virgin is built in the main square of Glossa, next to the taxi rank. It has a lovely peaceful atmosphere if you manage to escape inside from the traffic and confusion of the road to Loutraki, which passes alongside it. The views from the terrace are lovely, and you can enjoy them from the estiatoria or the café outside the church - but they are not as spectacular as those in the Eleftherotria church above.

Finally, we cannot end this chapter without a word about the importance of icons in the Orthodox religion.

Icons

The icon is of great importance to the Orthodox Christian. These beautiful and elaborate paintings are described as 'windows into the kingdom of God'. They are used in worship both in the decoration of the church and for private homes. The icon is seen as both a form of prayer and a means to prayer.

The icons painted on the walls of the churches throughout Greece are an early form of animation. They are a 'book' explaining the Orthodox faith for those unable to read.

Icons are not only revered in church: virtually every house contains an icon stand (iconostasis) containing various icons relevant to the family's history, as well as the wedding crowns. This is kept on a wall facing east, towards Constantinople. It is possible to guess the names of members of the family merely by looking at the icons displayed. Almost all personal names in Greece are shared in common with a Saint and, instead of birthdays, Saints' days are celebrated. In times of need a person may beseech these Saints for help. Perhaps the single most revered Saint in Greece is the Virgin Mary.

If you are interested in icons, Madro Travel on the Paralea of Skopelos Town, occasionally organizes workshops so that you might paint your own under the tutelage of Anthi Balsamaki, one of the most foremost authorities on icons in Greece and iconographer at the Benaki Museum in Athens. Check out their web site for details (http://madrotravel.gr/).

Anthi has a house in Skopelos Town and will eventually move back here full time. A graduate of the Athens School of Fine Arts (the icon painting workshop of K. Xynopoulos), she is in charge of the Benaki Museum icon painting workshop. To date, she has had eight solo shows: she has been responsible for the icon decoration of many churches in Greece and abroad; and her works are in many private collections. She is one of the few women icon painters permitted to paint the icons on church walls, having received a special dispensation to this end from the Ecumenical Patriarchate in Constantinople. She is the author of a series of books discussing the technique and the symbolic nature of images in Orthodox iconography.

One of the countless churches of Skopelos

Archaeological Sites

Skopelos has a long and varied history, stretching back over 30,000 years. Much prehistoric evidence has been lost, covered or lies undeveloped because of lack of money and resources. And much of this would involve marine archaeology, which is extremely hazardous and expensive. However, enough artefacts have been uncovered to suggest that Skopelos was inhabited since early man first walked these islands.

Sendukia

In the heart of the island, some 6 km north west of the town, close to the top of the highest mountain, Delfi, are these fascinating sarcophagi - four tombs chiselled into the rock, with their boulder lids next to them. It's not certain exactly how old these tombs are; some historians opt for Roman, whilst others believe they are Neolithic. Supporting the latter theory is the fact that they resemble Neolithic graves that have been found in Evia. They were looted in the 19th century. The graves can only be reached by foot (20 mins walk) and the route is complicated. It is marked by splodges of red paint and white painted arrows, but these can be difficult to find; so if you wish to visit Sendoukia it is advisable to use a map. The view from the graves is spectacular. Below you will see the monastery of Aghios Efstathios, the little hamlet of Karia, the sea, and Alonnisos. To get to Sendoukia, you will either need to be a keen walker - from town it should take around 2.5 hours - or have your own transport.

Stafilos

Archaeological findings show colonisation by the Cretans around 1600 BC; excavations in the area of Stafilos beach in 1936 uncovered a grave whose size was equivalent to those of the royal tombs of the Minoan civilisation. Among other treasures they found a very large golden sword thought to belong to the Cretan prince, Stafilos. He and his brother Peparithos founded cities at Stafilos, Knossa, the site of the current day town of Glossa, and at the site of the present-day main town. The island came to be known as Peparithos. The Cretans brought with them grain, olive trees and grapevines, which in turn brought prosperity to the island through the following centuries. The tomb is not able to be visited by the public.

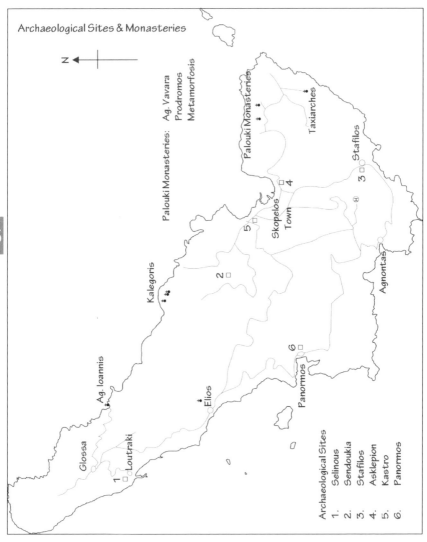

Map of the archaeological sites and monasteries

Roman Remains in Loutraki

Loutraki was known as Selinounda in Roman times and there are ruins all around the area, including Roman baths, remains of Athena's temple and a market place. The church is also built on the remains of an old temple. There is an information booth beside the car park by the harbour, which gives excellent information about the history of Loutraki and its surrounding areas.

The Asklepion Skopelos Town

Halfway around Skopelos Bay is the site of an ancient city. Digging has exposed a hospital/spa which was famous in classical time, the Asklepion.

The healing temples of Asklepios originated about the sixth century B.C. By the fourth century B.C. temples were in many places on the mainland and one had been built on Skopelos. These temples were extremely popular among both rich and poor. Rather than forerunners of hospitals, they seem to have been in modern terms a mixture of religious shrine and health spa.

Each Asklepieian temple was a conglomeration of buildings and areas, depending in size and opulence on its wealth and influence. The dominant structure was usually the main temple, in which a statue of the god was given a prominent place. Statues of various members of the family of Asklepios were often to be seen either in the temple or within its compounds. Somewhere in the precincts, on the entrance gates or before the portals, were tablets describing earlier miraculous cures and votive offerings which expressed gratitude for successful results. The dig on Skopelos has uncovered an important ancient well where many valuable offerings were found.

A round building, the tholos, contained water for purification, sometimes in a pool or, as here on Skopelos, bubbling from a sacred spring. Here, paintings and decorations were frequent.

The most important structure to the ailing suppliant was the incubation site, the abaton. This is what the dig has uncovered on Skopelos. All the preparations and anticipations were a prelude to what happened within the abaton, where the patient went to sleep until he was visited by the god. The actual cure took place in the worshiper's dreams.

The intention is to build a small museum on the archaeological site in order to display finds discovered during the dig, which has uncovered only a very small part of the original area. Unfortunately, most of this important classical site has disappeared under the sea.

The Kastro Skopelos Town

Although most visitors to Greece are rightly interested in its ancient and Classical past, it should not be forgotten that Venice played a role in Greece for nearly a thousand years. A possession of the Byzantine Empire, Venice gained political independence in the 8th century and later on became an independent Republic maintaining strict relationships with Constantinople.

In 1204, the Byzantine Empire was parcelled out among the leaders of the Fourth Crusade after they conquered Constantinople, but the small Aegean islands (including Skopelos) soon fell directly or indirectly into the hands of Venice: Skopelos was ruled by the Ghisi, a family of Venetian merchants, who were also given the islands of Mykonos and Tinos, among others.

In the 13th century, on the site of the ancient acropolis of Skopelos at the top of the hill, the Ghisi built a small fortress; not much more than a large tower. The Ghisi tower ensured control over the bay and it was protected by a maze of very narrow and steep streets, often interrupted by low arches. The Ghisi family in effect created a fortified town - the town *was* the fort - built upon the same principles as a castle with a double redout. This explains the winding streets, the numerous dead ends, bridges across houses and various strong fortified Venetian houses strategically placed around the town.

Venice had no large army, but had a powerful fleet, so the strategy to retain the Greek possessions was based on building fortresses which could resist the Turkish attack until help could arrive from the sea. To achieve this, in 1542 a Magistracy of Fortresses was established, which had jurisdiction over fortifications in the maritime and mainland dominions, and over the arsenals of sea territories of the Republic.

In Venice, the Ghisi family fell out of favour and on Skopelos their rule was replaced by absentee landlords, therefore allowing the town to fall into decline. In 1276 the island returned under the often nominal rule of the reconstituted Byzantine Empire.

The expansion of Venice continued until the Ottoman conquest of Constantinople in 1453. Afraid, the inhabitants of Skopelos requested Venetian protection.

Soon after that, the Sultans started a series of wars to gain possession of the Venetian bases. This process lasted more than three centuries. Only in 1715 with the fall of Tinos was the Aegean Sea freed from Venetian presence, but the Ionian Islands were retained by Venice until the Republic fell as a result of Napoleon's first Italian campaign.

Today the town of Skopelos occupies an area much larger than in the 15th century when it was under Venetian rule; the old town, however, is still easily identifiable, located on a low hill which sharply falls towards the modern town or towards the sea.

In 1538 Khayr al Din (Barbarossa - red beard), corsair and admiral of the Turkish fleet, seized Skopelos and destroyed the Kastro, reducing it to the ruin you see today.

Remains of the ruined Venetian fortress of Kastro

Flora and Fauna of Skopelos

For those who enjoy tranquility and a wide range of landscapes, Skopelos is an idyll. It is criss-crossed by a network of mule tracks and goat paths, which pass through dense pine forests, through olive groves where herds of goats graze, and tiny hamlets with picturesque country cottages. Along the way there are numerous wayside springs where you can quench your thirst.

Flora

For those interested in botany, the island boasts a huge range of flowers, trees and shrubs - around 700 species in total - providing colour and wonderful scents throughout the year. Around 67% of the island is covered by woodland: unlike the Cycladic islands, the Sporades are extremely green islands.

Skopelos has vast tracts of Aleppo pine forests, whose scent fills the air, and whose resin was collected and to flavour one of Greece's most famous products, retsina. Often, among the pines grow holm oak and heather, forming a sub-stratum, whilst small groves of plane trees grow along the banks of streams and dry river beds.

Elsewhere, the island is covered by tall, dense, almost impassable bushes of holm oak, heather, arbutus and lentisk. Brushwood, moss and wild flowers, such as daisies, Easter lilies, daffodils, marigolds, petrathias and iris are to be found all over the island in season. If you are interested in wildflowers, it's well worth visiting in April and early May as you will see a wide variety, including poppies, anemones, convulvulus, freesias, and gladioli. Many herbs, such as oregano, mint, basil and thyme grow wild.

The natural vegetation is interrupted by cultivated land with olive groves and orchards of plum, walnut, almond, orange and lemon trees. Vines are also cultivated.

Below the surface of the sea grows Poseidonia, the characteristic plant of the Mediterranean. It is of major importance to the underwater coastal eco-systems and constitutes an indicator of health of the marine environment.

Fauna

Birds

Just a look at the map of Greece gives a rough idea of the diversity of its fauna and flora. The geographical location and the variety of habitat types determine its rich bird life. The mainland is characterised by high mountains and very rugged relief alternating with small valleys and farmland. Freshwater lakes and coastal lagoons form an important network of wetlands. And of course, the island archipelagos; more than 2,000 islands, some big, like Crete, some small rocky islets, are the home of nesting seabirds and Eleonora Falcons.

Skopelos has a wide variety of fauna, including around 66 species of wild birds, native and migratory. There are several kinds of birds of prey: most common are the Eleonora Falcons (Falco eleonorae), the European Scops Owl (Otus scops), the Little Owl and the Common Buzzard (Buteo buteo). You may also be lucky enough to see kestrels, eagles, (golden and booted) buzzards and vultures. Along the coastlines, you can see grey herons, kingfishers, the great cormorants (Phalacrocorax carbo), the Herring gull (Larus argentatus) and the Yellow-legged Gull (Larus michahellis). Rare birds such as the gull Laurus auduinii are found here, along with colonies of black peregrine falcons, which nest in the cliffs. Severe winter weather can introduce rarely seen mainland birds temporarily. We have even had flamingos.

Garden and hedge birds include the Yellow Wagtail, the Willow Warbler, Redstart, Windchat, Bluetit, Robin, Nightingale and Spotted Flycatcher . Very obvious throughout the island is the Hooded Crow (Corvus cornix).

A large section of the area surrounding and including Mt. Palouki is posted as a no-hunting zone by the Skopelos Hunters' Association. Bird species missing from other parts of the island such as the Common Pheasant (Phasianus colchicus) and the Partridge have flourished in the protected area.

There is no tradition of ornithology in Greece. The Hellenic Ornithological Society (HOS), the local partner of Bird Life International, was founded only in 1982 but it saw a big period of growth during the 1990s. Its work is expanding all over the country. Although tourism is a very important source of foreign income, the State has never promoted bird-watching tourism.

Mammals

Skopelos is home to a rare breed of wild sheep - Skopelos Mavromatika

(Skopelos Blackeyes) - which have distinctive black rings around their eyes.

Wild land mammals include Pine Martens (Martes martes), Brown Rats (Rattus norvegicus) and mice, the Southern White-breasted Hedgehog (Erinaceus concolor), bats and, though declining in numbers, European Hares. There is also a type of ground squirrel known as an edible dormouse, as big as a rat with a pointy nose and a furry tail.

A mating pair of Fallow Deer (Dama dama) have been privately reintroduced to the island and you may occasionally see a wild boar in the north of the island.

An evolving population of feral cats exists in and around areas of human habitation.

Dolphins

According to Greek mythology, dolphins were originally fearsome pirates, who sailed the seas, took over other ships and killed the crews. One day a captain prayed to Dionysos, to turn him into a lion so that he could attack and kill the pirates. The god heard the sailor and granted his wish. The pirates, seeing the lion, repented of their misdeeds and prayed for forgiveness. Dionysos made them into dolphins, which, having great regrets for having killed so many sailors, now help them and escort them in their journeys. Dolphins would always escort Poseidon the sea god, whenever he was travelling on his golden cart, flying above the waves.

There is no better place than the seas of the Sporades and Skopelos if you want to observe one of the cleverest creatures that live in the water. Every local captain and sailor, especially those who live in Blo, has a story to tell about these magnificent creatures.

Sailing from the ports of Skiathos to Skopelos, you can often see dolphins playing near the front hull of the ferry. Sailors have been observing these wonderful creatures for centuries, as they accompany them on their journeys.

This specific behaviour of dolphins has never been scientifically explained. Many local people believe that their purpose is practical: that the ship's movement in the water offers an effortless ride for the dolphins, thus allowing them to save their strength. However dolphins never stay near the ship for too long, a fact that strengthens the view that dolphins just like to play around and have a great curiosity for people.

The skin of the dolphin is very sensitive and the movement in the water gives them a very pleasant sensation. We know for a fact that they love physical contact and that is why they like so much to swim having their body touching the ship's hull.

Dolphins belong to large mammals, like their close relatives, the whales. The first dolphins are alleged to have evolved some 65,000,000 years ago and experts say that they used to be large land mammals, who evolved into amphibians first and then into fish, in order to adapt to the sea.

A dolphin can jump as high as 3 metres above the water. Its teeth are conical and they are useful more for holding the food than cutting it. The dolphin has more teeth than any other mammal on earth. They feed at about the same time every day, and the feeding lasts for about an hour. In their groups an organized hierarchy is always noticeable.

Many people suffering from various serious illnesses, from depression to AIDS, have reported important changes, especially psychological and emotional, after their contact with dolphins. Plutarch once said:

"Dolphins are granted with the value that all philosophers seek: Selfless solidarity and friendship".

The Monk Seal

The Northern Sporades archipelago is one of the prime breeding areas of the Mediterranean Monk Seal (Monachus monachus), an endangered species. Monachus Seals are divided into three species: The Mediterranean seal Monachus monachus; The Hawaiian seal Monachus shcaunslandi; and the Caribbean seal Monachus tropicalis.

Man has accomplished the extinction of the Caribbean seals and brought the Hawaiian and Mediterranean seal to the verge of extinction. The Monk seal is the most rare of the seal species, one of the six most endangered animals on the planet and the number one endangered sea mammal in Europe.

The main threat to Monachus monachus is man and his activities. The relation between man and seal is often a competitive one. In Greece the main factor for the extinction of the seals is commercial fishing. The Monachus monachus seal which lives in the Greek seas is threatened by the lessening of the food available due to over-fishing and because of the accidental catch of seals in fishing nets. Additionally, industrial pollution and uncontrolled tourism cause the destruction of the natural habitat of seals, resulting in lower birth and higher death rates. Seals are at the top of the environmental pyramid, so their presence reflects the environmental health of the sea, while their extinction can be the foreteller of environmental destruction.

The Marine Park

Whilst staying on Skopelos or any of the Sporades Islands it is possible to organize a trip to the Marine Park, where it is feasible that you might see the Mediterranean seal Monachus monachus, dolphins and other creatures.

The cultural and biological importance of this area led the Greek state, in May 1992, to declare the area as environmentally protected, thus opening the National Marine Park; the first in Greece and one of the largest. It is designed to protect this species by restricting human encroachment on seal breeding areas.

Alonnisos, the island which is north of Skopelos, together with a number of smaller islands such as Peristera, Dio Aderfia, Skantsoura, Kyra Panagia, Youra, Psathoura and Piperi, accommodate the largest seal population in the world (estimated at around 300 seals) along with other endangered species like the Blackstone Hawk, the Aegean Seagull and the wild goat of Youra.

Reptiles and Amphibians

Skopelos is home to a variety of reptiles and amphibians. The Balkan Terrapin (Mauremys rivulata) can be found near fresh water along with the Greek Marsh Frog (Pelophylax kurtmuelleri) though this habitat is slowly disappearing due to development and destruction of the wetland areas. There are also European tree frogs (Hyla arborea) and Common Toads (Bufo bufo).

The Balkan Wall Lizard (Podarcis taurica) is seen regularly in daylight in warm weather and the Hemidactylus turcicus at night. A larger lizard is the Balkan Green Lizard (Lacerta trilineata). Wild tortoises can be seen, particularly on the approach to Agios Ioannis.

Several varieties of snakes can be observed: the Montpellier Snake (Malpolon monspessulanus), the Leopard Snake (Elephe situla), the Large Whip Snake (Coluber jugularis), the Grass Snake (Natrix natrix), and the Viper

(Viperidae ochia). Most of the snakes are not poisonous; only the viper poses a real danger but, as with most snakes, this is only when it is disturbed or provoked.

NB Many reptiles and amphibians can harbour Salmonella bacteria, so must be handled with caution - if at all!

A picturesque street in Skopelos Old Town

Agriculture

The economy of Skopelos is now fully dependent on the tourism industry which supports construction and other development-related industries. Though tourism is greatest during the summer months, Skopelos is also a year round retirement destination for Northern Europeans.

Agriculture, once a staple of the local economy, is in decline, though 2006 was a good year for olive oil production in Skopelos. Plum and almond orchards exist but are less extensive than in the past. Wine production from local grapes is minimal ever since the phylloxera blight of the 1940s destroyed the vineyards. Though there is some local small scale wine production using local grapes, most wine produced on the island is for home use and much is pressed from grapes imported from Thessaly.

Herding of domestic goats and domestic sheep continues and a local feta type cheese is produced from these stocks. Beekeeping and honey production have increased in recent years.

Skopelos supports a small fishing fleet which fishes local waters. Boats are small, usually tratas and gri-gri in which local fishermen go out overnight and from which they sell their catch in the morning. Restaurateurs get up early enough to have first choice and locals pick over what is left. Small trucks also patrol the villages selling fish from freezers in the back. The owners recite their wares through a megaphone or a microphone/speaker, which is the shouting usually to be heard in the mornings. There is also an excellent fish monger on the ring road opposite and just down from the fire-station. Should you buy fish from here, ask them to clean and prepare it for you – fish scales get everywhere in the kitchen! This is why you will often see people cleaning fish near the sea or on the harbour side.

(Fresh octopus is the devil to prepare – it has to be tenderised before you can cook it. However, I have now discovered that putting fresh octopus in the freezer overnight does the job for you, so you don't need to spend hours beating it over the head on rocks, or hitting it with a rolling pin!)

Local Food Production

Skopelos cannot support its population with locally produced food and goods. Most of what is used and consumed must be imported by ship from the mainland. Prices for food and consumer goods reflect the added expense of transportation. Most building materials, including sand, must also be imported. Gasoline and home heating fuel costs are, at minimum, five percent higher than on the mainland.

Almonds

Skopelos, with its many almond trees, has its own sweet made from almonds, 'hamalee' - a sugar-coated sweet - which is a speciality of the island. Buy it in the Ambrosia cake shop on the Paralea.

Walnuts

Due to the many walnut trees on the island, another special sweet is made locally, called 'karidopita', or walnut pie. It is often served with ice cream.

Prunes:

Oven or sun dried Blue or Red Plums. A very special sweet is chocolate coated plums, often stuffed with walnuts. Unfortunately, they are only made for a limited period – until the island plums run out! You can buy them at Alexandra's sweetshop in town.

Feta Cheese

A semi-soft, crumbly, well-salted white cheese made from goat's milk. Used in Skopelos cheese pie and other vegetable pies, added to salads and served with meals. The cheese factory is in the large creamy-yellow house situated down the steps from the ring road, before the turning to the Kastro.

Skopelos Cheese Pie

Not by definition a real pie, but a tiropita, a deep fried spiral of cheese stuffed filo dough. The pie is generally about 15cm in diameter and 3cm deep.

Olives and Olive Oil

Olive trees have an almost titanic resistance, a vital force which renders them almost immortal. Despite harsh winters and burning summers, despite truncations, they continue to grow, proud and strong, reaching towards the sky, bearing fruit that nourishes and heals, inspires and amazes.

To take a walk amongst the olive groves in Skopelos is indeed akin to stepping back in time. You can feel the knowledge, strength and wisdom of the olive tree all around you. Temperate climactic conditions, characterized by warm dry summers and rainy winters, favour plentiful harvests; stone, drought, silence and solitude are the ideal habitat for the majestic olive tree.

Today, Italy and Spain are the most prolific producers of olive oil, using the most advanced methods and sophisticated technologies, although Greece is the third largest producer and still very active for its size.

Olive groves occupy more than 14% of the cultivated land in Greece. Spread throughout the mainland and the islands, some 127,000 olive trees produce the fragrant light quality oil. Greece produces more than 300,000 tons of olive oil yearly and more than 70% of this oil is the desirable, low-acidic virgin and extra virgin types. This is a considerably higher yield of this kind of oil than found in the other Mediterranean countries. (In Italy it is less than 50% and in Spain, less than 30%). About one third of the total production (extra virgin and virgin) is exported to other countries. Approximately 50% of that is exported to other olive oil producing countries!

The viable olive orchards on Skopelos are carefully tended using organic methods - organic fertilizers are used, along with sustainable pest control, and natural irrigation.

Olive trees need little tender loving care, but they do need the right conditions for a bumper harvest. In March and April the trees are trimmed and fertilized. Trees bear fruit every two years and need the correct kind of wind in the blossom season to spread the pollen. Winds must be accompanied by dry weather and no frosts if there is to be a good crop.

As the olive fruit ripens, it changes colour from white to green and then to black. The people of Skopelos closely watch this ripening process and hand pick the olives at just the right time. After the long hot summer, with rains preferably at night, the olives are harvested in October/November. Timing depends on the season's rainfall.

Harvesting is an activity that involves the whole family and any friends that can be press-ganged into helping. First the ground is cleaned of twigs and debris, then nets are laid to catch the olives as they are scraped from the branches either with gloved or bare hands, or long bamboo sticks. More experienced pickers with strong upper arm muscles reach up to olives high in the treetops, whilst more fool-hardy people climb up into the upper branches to get at the top-most olives, some take the lower branches and others empty buckets of olives into the waiting sacks. The most difficult trees are the ones on the slopes, since the nets have to be held up on stakes to keep the olives from rolling off.

Once the olives are picked, they are taken to the olive press in Glossa, where the rest of the process is completed. The best part of helping your friends pick olives is that your payment is many litres of the most delicious oil as a show of gratitude!

Within a few hours, the olives are washed in cold water. The olives are only pressed once. Then the oil is immediately stored in clean stainless steel tanks. It is NEVER blended with oils from other sources. Olive oil from Skopelos is of high quality and tastes very different from the oil to be bought abroad.

Greeks first began pressing olives over 5,000 years ago and the principles of original methods are still used on Skopelos today, producing high quality olive oil. An olive press works by applying pressure to olive paste to separate the liquid oil and vegetation water from the solid material. The oil and vegetation water are then separated by standard decantation.

First the olives are ground into an olive paste using large millstones. Grindstones, while ancient in design, are a suitable way to grind olives, because this method breaks up the pulp while only slightly touching the nut and the skin. This reduces the release of the oxygenated enzymes present in these organs. Additionally, in this extraction method, the introduction of water is minimal when compared to the modern one, thus reducing the washing-off of the polyphenols. The exhausted paste, called pomace, has a low content of water, making it an easier residue to manage.

The olive paste generally stays under the stones for 30 to 40 minutes. This has three objectives:

- to guarantee that the olives are well ground
- to allow enough time for the oil to form the largest droplets
- to allow the fruit enzymes to produce some of the oil aromas and taste

After grinding, the olive paste is spread on fibre disks, which are stacked on top of each other, then placed into the press. Traditionally the disks were made of hemp or coconut fibre, but in modern times are made of synthetic fibres which are easier to clean and maintain.

These disks are then put on a hydraulic piston, forming a pile. Pressure is applied on the disks, thus compacting the solid phase of the olive paste and percolating the liquid phases (oil and vegetation water). The applied hydraulic pressure can go to 400 atm.

To facilitate separation of the liquid phases, water is run down the sides of the disks to increase the speed of percolation.

The liquids are then separated either by a standard process of decantation or by means of a faster vertical centifruge.

The traditional method is a valid form of producing high quality olive oil, if after each extraction the disks are properly cleaned from the remains of paste; if not the leftover paste will begin to ferment, thereby producing inconsistencies of flavors (called defects) that will contaminate the subsequently produced olive oil. A similar problem can affect the grindstones that, in order to assure perfect quality, also require cleaning after each usage. Proper cleaning produces higher quality oil.

On Skopelos, these methods require more manual labour and there is a longer time period from harvest to pressing. This non-continuous process with waiting periods exposes the olive paste to the action of oxygen and light. Even so, the oil produced is of excellent quality.

We treasure the extra-virgin oil types for their nutritional and salutary virtues. Extra-virgin oil is the most digestible of the edible fats; it helps to assimilate vitamins A, D and K; it contains so called essential acids that cannot be produced by our own bodies; it also slows down the aging process; and it helps bile, liver and intestinal functions. It is also valued for its culinary virtues and organoleptic properties of flavour, bouquet and colour! The best way to sample some of the locally produces oil is to simply drizzle a little on to some freshly baked bread - delicious! Why not try it and see!

What makes a great eating olive?

Do not let anyone tell you that one olive is much the same as another and there are no differences. Any olive lover will know to look at the following criteria; ripening, handling, size, grading and sorting, quality, curing, colour and brine.

The best olives are ripened naturally and hand-picked, allowing for extra large and unblemished fruits. They should be variable in colour, reflecting the olive's natural beauty. Olives that are harvested before they are ripe and picked mechanically have not reached full maturity and therefore do not have their natural, full flavour.

The olives should then ideally be salt-cured for 3-12 months in a pH-balance controlled environment with continuous rinsing.

The brine should be fresh made with top quality ingredients and only marinades with high acidity vinegar and oil should be used. Extra virgin olive oil should also be used, to further preserve the fruit.

If they are cured too quickly for production's sake, this will affect the taste and colour. The olives will all be black, reflecting oxidation and contact with the air.

Some of the best olives are found in huge open tins in the supermarkets, simply waiting to be bought and tasted!

Lemons

'Her garden has only lemon trees, her cologne has the smell of lemon, her dresses contain all possible gradations from unripe to mature sour fruit, she cooks special meat with lemon juice and the home-made lemonade is always available to the visitor during summer time'. This is how the ladies of Skopelos were described in the nineteenth century.

The lemon is a cultivating hybrid coming from wild varieties such as citrus and mandarin. It is not known where and when this genetic variety was realized. Citrus, the fruit which Plinios refers to as malum medicum – the 'medical fruit' - is the first hesperid known in the Mediterranean.

Lemon trees can grow up to 6 metres (20 feet) in height, but usually grow less. 'She did not grow up, she is like the short lemon tree', used to be said on Skopelos about women who were short.

The branches of the lemon tree have thorns and they have the shape of an open crown. The leaves are green, bright and of elliptic shape and the flowers are white with a light purple color inside. The flowers and the fruits of the lemon tree grow at the same time. The lemons are egg-shaped with sharp edges, the mature fruits having a bright yellow color.

Lemon trees grow in tropical and mild climates and do not bear very low temperatures. They need temperatures of between 15-30°C (60-85°F) and sunny weather, growing well in fertile dry ground. Lemon trees need a lot of water, but it is necessary to keep the ground dry between waterings.

Two main factors which make these trees grow well in this area is the climate on the one hand, and the water of Skopelos on the other. The water on the island does not contain medicinal salts and boron, which are injurious for lemon trees.

The lemon tree grows more than any other hesperid and gives thousands of fruits yearly. Nevertheless it is a very sensitive tree and can suffer from 'kommiosis', which usually kills it. The trees need a lot of care: weeding, four or five manures, organic manures, pruning, sprinkling etc. Eight to ten times yearly fruit is selected for export, beginning in September and finishing in February.

Figs

The fig-tree is one of the first trees which man cultivated on earth (7,000 B.C. in Jericho). It is the first tree mentioned in the Bible, while in India it is considered to be a holy tree.

There are many references in the Greek mythology to the Fig-tree. It was worshipped as a tree belonging to Dionysos and to Priapus, directly related to the 'infernal' energy for reproduction, fertility and the eternal flow of nature. According to another version, the Fig-tree was offered as a gift by Demeter to the people living in Attica, where Demeter had resorted when she was grieving for the carrying away of Persephone by Hades.

The particular relation of the Fig-tree to the 'gods' of earth, to dust, to water and to mud, is clearly shown in its form. Its wood is grey, the same colour of stones, it is porous and it is not burned easily. It is moist and is totally resin-free. The Fig-tree bears fruit even in periods of drought, as it keeps humidity in its wood. It produces a kind of milk instead of resin. The milk of the fig-tree is lightly caustic and causes itching and irritation.

The fig-tree has no buds which bloom, nor has it any colourful flowers in order to attract insects and be fertilized and make fruits. The fig-tree blooms 'inside' the small inflated sachets, the figs, which are full of stamens, small seeds and juice. If not collected, they attract the insects due to their sweetness, then rot and fall to the ground. Fig-trees are 'easy' trees, as they sprout everywhere, in precipices or stony ground and even in areas very close to the sea.

August is the time to harvest figs. They should be collected early in the morning, then left in the sun. In order to avoid any worms they are scalded with water aromatized with oregano, laurel and fennel. After drying, the figs are put into cartons with laurel leaves.

Some fig-trees give black-figs, being dark and soft, while some others give white figs, which are shiny and have a light-green colour.

Dried figs are sweet like honey, aromatic like the finest perfume, and satisfying like the most delicious food. Open the fig in the middle so that the stalk can keep the two pieces together, put an almond or a walnut inside, close the fig and eat it slowly!

Plums

The common plum is the scientific name of the plum tree, the fruit tree which gives us the purple, or sometimes red or golden, fruit. There are more than 2,000 plums which differ in size, shape, color and taste. The darker plums have a more bitter peel, while red and yellow ones are more sweet. Most plums that can be eaten fresh can also be cooked and contain more antioxidants than any other fruit.

Plums were first cultivated in Asia. They are mentioned in the writings of Confucius in 479 A.D. and were included in the kitchen of ancient Chinese civilization. The plum tree has an important role in Chinese mythology and is associated with wisdom and spiritual maturity. Alexander the Great brought plums to the Mediterranean and Gaius Pompeius introduced them to the gardens of Rome.

In Greece the most common variety is the Azen, which is mainly cultivated in Skopelos. Plums have a sweet, rich taste which is excellent with the traditional cooking of the Greek countryside. They are usually eaten dried and that is the most common form to be found in the market.

Dry prunes are made in many ways. You can let them dry on the tree, but they are usually left in trays in the sunlight. You can also put them in the stove on a low heat. There are many old plum ovens still extant around Skopelos.

Dry prunes are not only good for indigestion but are also great for hangovers. They provide energy and are also believed to be an aphrodisiac. In Skopeliti folk tradition, if you see an immature plum not on a tree, it means that you or your relatives will be in a bad mood. If the plums are mature then you will have short-lived pleasure. If you dream of eating plums then many joyful things will happen, but they too will not last long. If you are picking plums from the ground and some are bad, this means the co-existence of bad times among good ones. A plum tree that has many leaves means you will benefit financially.

Prunes are used in salty recipes, mainly from Middle East, and are a very good side dish for pork and chicken.

Honey

Honey is a thick syrup, having a deep amber colour, scented and with a sweet taste which is much better than sugar. It is produced by bees as they collect flower or fruit nectar from living parts of plants or honey dews from other insects. They then carry this nectar to their hive, where it is made into honey. The honey is then stored by the bees inside their honeycombs, where it matures. Finally, the bees create a moisture-proof seal for the honeycomb.

Honey has a long history in Greece - Zeus first used honey on Mount Olympus. Early forms of honey collecting entailed the destruction of the entire colony when the honey was harvested. The wild hive was crudely broken into, using smoke to suppress the bees, the honeycombs were torn out and smashed up - along with the eggs, larvae and honey they contained. The liquid honey from the destroyed brood nest was crudely strained through a sieve or basket. This was destructive and unhygienic, but for hunter-gatherer societies this did not matter, since the honey was generally consumed immediately and there were always more wild colonies to exploit.

However, in settled societies the destruction of the bee colony meant the loss of a valuable resource; this drawback made beekeeping both inefficient and something of a 'stop - start' activity. There could be no continuity of production and no possibility of selective breeding, since each bee colony was destroyed at harvest time, along with its precious queen. Since sugar was a product unknown for ancient civilizations, honey was essential for their diet and of course an important ingredient for making sweets. Honey for ancient peoples was a gift sent by the gods, since they believed it fell from the heavens every morning onto the leaves of the flowers, so that the bees could then collect it.

The therapeutic agents of honey were well known, and that is why beekeeping was active in many places, especially in Greece and Egypt. Thousands of years ago, humans began to domesticate wild bees in artificial hives made from hollow logs, wooden boxes, pottery vessels, and woven straw baskets or 'skeps'. The walls of the sun temple of Nyuserre Ini, from the 5th Dynasty, before 2422 BC, depicts workers blowing smoke into hives as they are removing honeycombs. Honey played an important role in the lives of ancient people. They used to fill large pots with honey mixed with wine as an offering to the gods and the souls of their dead.

In prehistoric Greece (Crete and Mycenae), bee keeping was systemic, as can be seen in the finds of hives, smoking pots, honey extractors and other beekeeping paraphernalia in Knossos. Beekeeping was considered a highly valued industry controlled by beekeeping overseers - owners of gold rings depicting bee keeping scenes.

During the medieval period abbeys and monasteries were centres of beekeeping, since beeswax was highly prized for candles and fermented honey was used to make alcoholic mead in areas of Europe where vines would not grow.

The 18th and 19th centuries saw successive stages of a revolution in beekeeping, which allowed the bees themselves to be preserved when taking the harvest. This revolution in beekeeping practice was completed through the perfection of the movable comb hive by Lorenzo Lorraine Langstroth, a descendant of Yorkshire farmers who emigrated to the United States.

He designed a series of wooden frames within a rectangular hive box, carefully maintaining the correct space between successive frames, and found that the bees would build parallel honeycombs in the box without bonding them to each other or to the hive walls. This enables the beekeeper to slide any frame out of the hive for inspection, without harming the bees or the comb, protecting the eggs, larvae and pupae contained within the cells. It also meant that combs containing honey could be gently removed and the honey extracted without destroying the comb. The emptied honey combs could then be returned to the bees intact for refilling.

Honey in Skopelos is mainly pine honey from conifer trees, chestnut honey and flower-honey from the nectar of fruit trees and wild flowers such as thyme.

Pine Honey

Pine honey has a very special scent, which some people liken to the scent of iodine. The colour of the pine honey is darker than thyme honey. Pine honey produced during Spring is brighter and clearer than honey produced during the Autumn.

Pine honey extracts its sugar rather slowly, since it is low in glucose. It is a honey of high nutritional value since it contains minerals and micro-nutrients such as calcium, magnesium, zinc, iron and copper.

Chestnut Honey

This is produced from the nectar and honey dews of the chestnut tree, a very common tree throughout Northern Greece and the Sporades. It has a lasting, strong, mildly bitter taste. Its colour varies depending upon its origin from light brown to dark brown and black. It crystallizes slowly after 1-2 years and it is very rich in micro-nutrients.

Blossom Honey

This is produced from flower nectar. Among the blossom honeys are the thyme and orange tree honey. Thyme honey is very aromatic and crystallizes within 6 to 18 months from production.

Domesticated Animals

The land area of Greece is 35% semi-mountainous and 57% mountainous, a total of 92 percent. Not surprisingly, the cow population of Greece is only 800,000, while goats number close to 6 million and sheep more than 10 million - for only 10 million people. Total milk production per person per year is higher in other countries. However, of world production of sheep milk and goat milk, Greece produces 8% of the former and 4% of the latter despite having only 2% of the world's sheep and goat population. This makes Greece unique among the dairy countries of the world. Additionally, cheese consumption per person per year in Greece is 52lb - by far greater than in any other country.

Chickens, turkeys, geese and rabbits are raised for family consumption.

Skopelos Goat

The island has its own indigenous acknowledged breed of goat named the 'Skopelos'. The Skopelos goat is a breed in the Southern Multicoloured Group. It is a relative of the wild goat of the island of Gioura. Unicoloured goats are red or brown, multicoloured are black, red, brown and white. Some have special characteristics: they are red brownish coloration with white spots on the flank and back. Because they are so large, Skopelos goats yield a good profit and a good farm income.

Goats originate in the highlands of western Iran, and were one of the earliest of animals to be domesticated. The goat is a very hardy animal, able to digest almost any food. Relatively docile, it is easy to raise, and each female usually produces twins. Hence, the goat provides meat not just for the people of Skopelos, but also for millions of people all over the world, and it has done so for at least 10,000 years.

Skopelos Sheep

Sheep herds on the island belong to a distinctive group called the 'Skopelos Sheep' breed. This is a prolific dairy sheep breed in Greece. All parts of the sheep are utilized, and it is a main source of wealth. Sheep's head is a delicacy served in northern Europe, in many Muslim countries and most places where sheep are raised and is served roasted and/or boiled. This is the delicacy loved by all during feast days, when whole animals are roasted on the spit.

Dogs

Most dogs are kept outdoors and are used as guard dogs for farm property. Some of these are pointing breeds used as bird dogs during the hunting season. Varro, writing in *De Re Rustica* (37 BC), a treatise on farming whose principals are still extant today on Skopelos, recognizes *"two sorts of dogs - the hunting-dog suited to chase the beasts of the forest, and the other which is procured as a watch-dog and is of importance to the shepherd"*. He speaks only of the sheep dog, which should be *"large, with a deep bark, and white in colour so as to be more easily recognized in the dark. To protect the neck from the bite of wolves, it should wear a nail-studded leather collar"*. Later, an all-white dog is recommended for the shepherd to avoid mistaking it for a wolf in the half-light of dawn or dusk, and an all-black guard dog for the farm to terrify thieves in the daytime and be less visible to intruders at night.

Working donkeys on the island usually have their own guard dog - watch out for them when you are driving.

Many older Skopelitians regard dogs (and cats) as vermin and react as many other people might do to a rat.

Older gentleman of Skopelos with his komboloi (worry beads)

Useful Contacts

Information

www.madrotravel.com - accommodation, travel, culture and tradition

www.skopelosnet.com - real estate and accommodation

www.skopelosweb.gr - live web cam Skopelos Town and Glossa

www.skopelitissa.com - the Norwegian connection - a personal diary

www.Skopelos.TripAdvisor.co.uk - FAQ about Skopelos answered

www.meteo.gr/stations/skopelos - current weather conditions including storm warnings

www.openseas.gr - information about ferry schedules

Holiday Companies

Sunvil Holidays	www.sunvil.co.uk
Greek Islands Club	www.greekislandsclub.com
Islands of Greece	www.islands-of-greece.co.uk
Ionian/Aegean	www.ionianislandholidays.com
Thomsons Holidays	www.thomson.co.uk
Thalpos Holidays	www.holidayislands.com
Manos	www.ThomasCook.com
Olympic Holidays	www.OlympicHolidays.com

Bus Travel

KTEL bus company	www.ktelvolou.gr
Athens	+30 210 6329585/8317186
Volos	+30 24210 33254/25527
Thessaloniki	+30 2310 595424
Alkyon Travel	www.alkyontravel.gr
Athens	+30 210 3843202
Aghios Konstantinos	+30 22350 31059

Tourist Companies on Skopelos

Madro Travel	+30 24240 22300/22145
	email: info@madrotravel.com

Thalpos Travel   +30 24240 29036/23295
                       email: info@holidayislands.com
Dolphin of Skopelos   +30 24240 29191-2
                       email: info@dolphinofskopelos.com
Lemonis Agency   +30 24240 22363

Accommodation on Skopelos

Madro Travel   +30 24240 22300/22145
                       email: info@madrotravel.com
Room Rental Association   +30 24240 22712
Thalpos Travel   +30 24240 29036/23295
                       email: info@holidayislands.com

Flying Cat/dolphin/ferry ticket agencies

ATHENS

Hellenic Seaways: Alkyon Travel, 97 Akadimias Str, Kaningos Square, Athens
                       +30 210 3843202,
                       +30 210 3832545 Fax +30 210 3843220

Hellas Flying Dolphins: Booking Centre, 98-100, Sigrou Ave, Athens 117 41
                       +30 210 4199000
                       www.hellenicseaways.gr

AGHIOS KONSTANTINOS

Hellenic Seaways: Bilalis Nikolaos, 4, Karaiskaki str., 350 06 Ag. Constantinos
                       +30 22350 31614
                       +30 22350 31874 Fax +30 22350 31874 www.bta.gr

VOLOS

Hellenic Seaways   : **Sporades Travel**, 32, Argonauton str., 382 21, Volos
                       +30 24210 23415
                       +30 24210 35846   Fax: +30 24210 35846

THESSALONIKI

Hellenic Seaways: **Zorpidis Tourism Organisation**
                       4, Salaminos str, Thessaloniki
                             +30 2310 555995   Fax: 30 2310 555475
                       Email : reservations@zorpidis.gr

SKOPELOS

Hellenic Seaways: Nautical Agency Skopelos, Skopelos Port

+30 24240 22767   +30 24240 23060

Fax +30 4240 23608

SPEEDCAT/NEL LINES: Madro Travel, Paralea, Skopelos

+30 24240 22300/22145

Fax:+30 24240 22941

SPEEDCAT: Lemonis Agency, Paralea, Skopelos   +30 24240 22363

Olympic Air Reservations +30210 3550500 / 8018010101(within Greece)

Other Agencies

Volos: Vis Travel   +30 24210 31059   www.gtp.gr/VIS-travel

Athens: Flash Tours   +30 210 3300404

Yacht hire

www.odysseysailing.gr/islands.html

Sailing Flotilla holidays

www.sunsail.co.uk

Port Authorities

Port Authority of Skopelos   +30 24240 22180

Port Authority of Glossa   +30 24240 33033

Boat hire

Madro Travel   +30 24240 22145

Thalpos   +30 24240 29036

Health Care

Health Centre +30 24240 22222   +30 24240 22739   +30 24240 22592

Peripheral Infirmary of Glossa   +30 24240 33504

Peripheral infirmary of Elios/Klima   +30 24240 33000

Dentists:

Ioannis Radamantis	+30 24240 22862
Giorgos Tsarpalas	+30 24240 22208

Pharmacies:

Radamantis (in Platonos Square)	+30 24240 22666
	+30 24240 22252
Tsarpalas (opposite medical centre)	+30 24240 24333

Private Practice: Dr I Skaventzos   +30 699 99 2455

Public Services

Fire Station – Skopelos		+30 24240 22768
Police Station - Skopelos	+30 24240 22235	+30 24240 22988
Post Office – Skopelos		+30 24240 22203
Post Office – Glossa		+30 24240 33555

Banks

National Bank	+30 24240 22224
Agrotiki	+30 24240 22384
Commercial	+30 24240 22700
Alpha Bank	+30 24240 24215

Internet

The Blue Sea Cafe bar and internet cafe, Paralea, Skopelos Town

+30 24240 23010.

Vehicle hire

There are many places from which to hire cars and motorbikes in Skopelos Town: most of them are situated on the new port end of the Paralea, both at the beginning of the road around the bay and on the short road from the port to the T junction. Below are the biggest companies:

Discovery Cars	+30 24240 22198	FAX	+30 24240 22941
Magic Cars	+30 24240 23250	FAX	+30 24240 22198
Motor Tours	+30 24240 22986	FAX	+30 24240 22602

Bicycle hire

Skopelos Cycling   +30 24240 22398

email skopeloscycling@yahoo.gr

Pony trekking

Apaloosa Valley Yurts - contact Libby   +30 75944 38753

Email: admin@appaloosavalleyyurts-Skopelos.com

Maps

Skopelos Topo Touring & Hiking Map 10.12; Publisher: Anavasi

ISBN: 9789608195226; Series: Anavasi Island Maps

Language: Greek, English & French; Format: Folded Map, Scale 1:25000

GPS friendly; www.anavasi.gr

Buy from Madro Travel, Paralea, Skopelos

Charitable Organisations of Skopelos

FAROS charity for people with terminal illness on Skopelos

                                        www.farosskopelou.gr

MoM Hellenic monk seal society;   www.mom.gr

SCAN animal welfare   www.scanskopelos.org

Cultural Association of Skopelos   www.skopelosculture.com

British Embassy, Athens   +30 201 727 2600